The New Uprooted

THE NEW UPROOTED

Single Mothers in Urban Life

ELIZABETH A. MULROY

Foreword by Philip W. Johnston

AUBURN HOUSE
Westport, Connecticut • London

Library of Congress Cataloging-in-Publication Data

Mulroy, Elizabeth A.
    The new uprooted : single mothers in urban life / Elizabeth A.
  Mulroy ; foreword by Philip W. Johnston.
       p.   cm.
    Includes bibliographical references and index.
    ISBN 0–86569–038–3 (hc : alk. paper).— ISBN 0–86569–039–1 (pbk.:
  alk. paper)
    1. Single mothers—United States—Social conditions. 2. Poor
  women—United States. 3. Single-parent family—United States.
  4. Family policy—United States. 5. Urban poor—United States.
  6. Urban policy—United States. 7. United States—Social
  conditions—1980– I. Title.
  HQ759.915.M85   1995
  306.85'6'0973—dc20   95–2084

British Library Cataloguing in Publication Data is available.

Library of Congress Catalog Card Number: 95–2084
ISBN: 0–86569–038–3
    0–86569–039–1 (pbk.)

First published in 1995

Auburn House, 88 Post Road West, Westport, CT 06881
An imprint of Greenwood Publishing Group, Inc.

Printed in the United States of America

The paper used in this book complies with the
Permanent Paper Standard issued by the National
Information Standards Organization (Z39.48–1984).

10 9 8 7 6 5 4 3 2 1

Dedicated to my mother
Dorothy
with love and appreciation

Contents

List of Figures

Foreword

As one listens to the stern lectures to poor, single mothers emanating from the mouths of affluent, powerful male politicians these days, one can only conclude that they represent a particularly vicious and mean-spirited strain in the American psyche. After all, on the face of it, single mothers hardly pose the threat to the stability of our society as portrayed by lecturing politicians: only 1 percent of the federal budget goes to finance the Aid to Families with Dependent Children (AFDC) program and, contrary to popular mythology, a relatively small percentage (5 percent) of women receiving AFDC are teenagers. Moreover, these women who are the objects of assaultive rhetoric at least are accepting parenting responsibilities while, in too many cases, the men who fathered their children have disappeared from the scene.

American historians have written about the unique perspective our culture has on people who live in poverty: we have divided them into two groups—"the deserving poor" and "the undeserving poor." This perspective holds that the deserving poor are poor through no fault of their own and because of conditions over which they have no control, like the elderly or the physically and mentally disabled. The undeserving poor, on the other hand, are perceived to have actively participated in their drop to the bottom of the economic ladder and are, in large part, responsible for their impoverishment. This group includes unwed mothers, substance abusers, and people who have contracted diseases through risky behavior. The public policies that relate to the two groups differ radically in their generosity.

Most other industrialized nations consider it to be in their country's interest to provide assistance to low-income children so that they will become healthy, independent, taxpaying members of the society. Regrettably, the United States has a dismal record in this regard. It is no accident that the United Kingdom, France, Germany, the Netherlands, and Sweden all lift over 70 percent of low-income children out of poverty through government benefits, while the figure in the United States is a shocking 8.5 percent. The moral judgment that divides America's low-income individuals into two quite distinct groups is not a factor in most other nations. My observation is that the only way to explode the mythology regarding poor, single women—"the undeserving poor"—is through the constant repetition of well-documented facts.

In this book, Elizabeth Mulroy makes a significant contribution to our understanding of the vast array of pressures on single mothers in the modern era. By examining the failure of many fathers to support their children, the pervasive violence in the lives of many poor women and their children, the limited employment options that are available, and the frequent inability of many single mothers to pay for decent housing in safe neighborhoods, Mulroy underscores the daily stresses of trying to survive as a mother alone within the context of a society where rules are largely hostile to her and her family—a society that foolishly fails to see all children as "our" children.

One example of how this book illustrates public policy considerations is Mulroy's discussion of the impact of domestic violence on young women. Many states are now adopting laws that require teen mothers to remain living with their parents as a condition for receiving AFDC benefits. Yet, the data suggests that a very significant number (40 percent) of such women are the victims of sexual abuse by a male member of the household. Therefore, on the surface, what appears to be a sensible, rational policy to eliminate any financial incentive for teenagers to become pregnant is much more complex and murky—even dangerous—when considered within the context of Mulroy's exposition on domestic violence drawn from the real experiences of single mothers themselves.

Similarly, the typical single mother's often desperate search for affordable housing in a neighborhood providing a real measure of physical safety is a problem often ignored by public policymakers. While the media portrays the young and single mentally ill or substance abusing male as the stereotypical homeless person, the reality is that large numbers of families experience homelessness as well. As Mulroy points out, federal housing policies during the Reagan and Bush administrations essentially destroyed the federal commitment to help subsidize housing for the poor. In many cities throughout the country, this means that low-income women and their children—often without family support—are forced to choose between unsafe public housing projects and the streets.

The cumulative effect of this disorder on children is devastating. Exposed to violence within the family early in life, then feeling threatened by their immediate outside environment throughout childhood and adolescence, many poor children hope simply to survive until the next day. Furthermore, these children suffer emotional wounds when they realize that the men who fathered them care so little for them and their mothers that they refuse to help financially. As some national leaders have pointed out, it takes a village to raise a child. Yet too often in our society the village demonizes and undercuts the one adult trying to protect the child—the mother. Seen through a child's eyes, the mother's source of isolation and desperation must also be the child's. And therein lies the illumination of Mulroy's message: as we undermine the mother, so do we undermine the child. As public policies become increasingly punitive towards single mothers, we are sealing the fate of their children, who will have a difficult time succeeding in society. If we fail to respond to the crisis of domestic violence, the lack of affordable housing, and non-existent or insufficient child support, we make it far more difficult for the remaining parent to fulfill her most important job—to parent. Scholars and social critics have observed the irony—even the hypocrisy—of society's message: middle-class women should be home with their children, while poor women should leave their children during the day and go to work. Thus, many states are adopting workfare laws which require women on welfare to find jobs, often without child care or job training.

Despite the $34 billion in uncollected child support, nobody is proposing a work requirement for the fathers, only for the mothers. This is the worst kind of misogyny on the part of politicians who are tapping into the outrage many working people feel about the notion that welfare permits people to get something for doing nothing. As usual, the political debate over welfare reform focuses on the women; rarely, if ever, do the politicians talk about the responsibilities of the men who fathered the children on AFDC. Having been involved in this issue for a quarter century, I am convinced that the welfare controversy will not be resolved until we hold fathers accountable for the consequences of their actions and help them to become active participants in the lives of their children.

Mulroy concludes her assessment of poor families in America today by making a series of recommendations to policymakers. She understands that acting on these recommendations is important to the mothers and children she writes about in this book. But, in a larger sense, she also realizes that action is imperative for the broader society. If low-income families could escape poverty, the creative energy let loose would be a great boon to our entire nation. Consider that one in four children today lives in poverty. Imagine what our country would be like if those millions of children were able to grow and thrive like other children. Then they could play important roles in all areas of our national life and we would all benefit. I cannot think of a wiser investment in our future. *The New Uprooted* gives us a road map to that future. I hope we have the foresight and the courage to follow it.

June 1995
Boston, Mass.

Philip W. Johnston
New England Director
United States Department of
Health and Human Services

Part I

Background

Part I consists of three chapters that introduce the topic of single-parent families in the context of urban life in the 1990s. Chapter 1, an introduction, offers a theoretical framework and rationale for the approach selected. Chapter 2 analyzes explanatory factors for thirty years of changing family form of which the rise in one-parent families is but one of many changes in household composition. National demographic and economic data are examined relative to the effects of economic restructuring on changes in family economic support. Finally, Chapter 3 examines historical changes in urban development and in federal housing policies. This analysis provides the basis for understanding the context of single-parent living environments—the nexus where a family's social and physical worlds intersect—with repercussions for individual choices, behavior, and family well-being.

—1—

Introduction

In her July, 1993, confirmation hearing for appointment to The United States Supreme Court, a Senator asked 60-year-old Judge Ruth Bader Ginsburg if she believed women interpret the law differently from men. She replied, "Women do not interpret the law differently, Senator. They *experience life* differently."[1]

The increased diversity in family form and the changing roles of women in society are among the most profound changes in the past quarter century in the United States. If the task of social science research is to contribute to the critique of existing forms of society (Giddens, 1984), this task has become a daunting one. Not only has family composition changed dramatically, but also the impacts of urbanization—the shift from rural to urban living—and the growth of a new American poverty have profoundly affected *how* families live.

One key trend at the center of a controversial national public debate is the increase in the number of families headed by women alone. One in four children in the United States is growing up in a one-parent family. Eighty-six percent of one-parent families are headed by women, and 14 percent are headed by men. They may be separated, divorced, or never-married. Increasingly, families headed by mothers are more concentrated—and more isolated—in central cities.

Who *are* single-parent families in the 1990s? What is their quality of life, their life choices and chances? What are their basic needs, and how do they meet them? To answer these questions, we use a broad lens. The purpose of this book is to examine how single mothers from a diverse set of social and economic circumstances experience dual roles of sole family breadwinner and sole resident parent in the changing urban environment of the 1990s. Families headed by mothers alone have become a unit of concern not only because they represent changing family form, but also because their current economic marginality threatens a downward spiral toward the instability of urban poverty. Their key settlement issue is the high cost of housing their families in relation to economic instability of low wages, irregular or nonpayment of child support, and welfare benefit levels. The trauma of domestic violence contributes additional personal instability, stress, and insecurity to millions of women and their children.

While much has been written about family relations, divorce, teen pregnancy, and welfare reform, very little is known about the day-to-day experiences of single parents themselves or the details of their living conditions. There is little systematic research on who these mothers are, why they make the choices they make, and what the consequences are of their decisions.

The news and entertainment media often portray single-parent families as a public symbol for a plethora of social problems: inner-city crime and violence, deterioration of urban neighborhoods, the budget deficit, school dropout rates, and educational failure. Contrary to the stereotypical layabout welfare mom, the vast majority of single mothers are productive citizens who labor hard to support their families under stressful conditions and without available supports. Faced with the economic necessity of supporting themselves and their children, 79 percent of single mothers with children between the ages 6 and 17 and 58.8 percent of those with children under 6 are employed.[2] The majority of single mothers, however, are still poor. Their median income is $13,100—about half the $26,000 in a single-father family and only one-third the $41,300 of a two-parent family with children.[3]

While the level of household income is a very important indicator of a family's level of well-being, a focus only on economic and social problems of one-parent families overlooks personal and community *assets* that strongly influence how one-parent families live. Which personal, neighborhood, and institutional factors facilitate a stable family life for them, and which hinder it? The changing social context of the environments in which they live is a critical force to be considered.

Although one-parent families are a diverse group and live throughout metropolitan and rural areas, those who live in central cities are raising children in increasingly distressed neighborhood conditions. The new poverty reflects a reversal of America's role as a melting pot society. Instead of absorption, today we observe separation. That is, social segmentation, economic inequality, and geographic isolation keep those who are perceived to be different further apart.[4]

The growth of the suburbs brought the middle class out of cities. Business and industry followed, leaving behind the working class and those in poverty. The restructuring of the economic base and the shift from industrial production to high-technology manufacturing has drastically changed the nature of work and employment possibilities for men and women. Waves of immigration in the 1970s and 1980s brought newcomer populations to urban neighborhoods vacated by the socially mobile middle class. Decreasing urban investment, deteriorating public facilities and infrastructure, increasing crime and violence have all impacted the changed character of cities and of urban residential neighborhoods. Family instability, dislocation, and disintegration should not be a surprising spillover effect from the force of these multiple and significant trends.

UNDERSTANDING BASIC NEEDS

In order to develop useful responses to the economic marginality of single-parent families at the individual, community, or policy levels, it is first necessary to understand what the basic needs of one-parent families are, and how and why they are interrelated. One influential and widely applied theory of basic needs was developed by Abraham Maslow who suggested that human behavior is motivated by a hierarchy of human needs that must be satisfied in a given order. Basic needs must be met first so that higher level needs can then be realized. According to Maslow, a hierarchy of needs includes, from lowest to highest, (1) physiological needs at the level of basic survival; (2) needs for physical safety and freedom from pain or fear; (3) needs for belonging, love, and social interaction; (4) self-esteem and status needs; and (5) self-actualization needs. Maslow's theories are taught as a humanistic approach to personality with wide application to theories of human motivation. Certain assumptions implicit in this model do not work, however, when applied to single-parent families. First, when women take concrete action to leave an abusive domestic relationship, they often give up the physical security of a home with a spouse or partner (Maslow's level 1) in order to achieve level 2, the need for physical safety and freedom from pain or fear. Families are the fastest growing population of the homeless, and battered women's shelters are often the only refuge for women and children who seek to escape domestic violence.

Figure 1.1
Potential Stresses on One-Parent Families: Family Instability

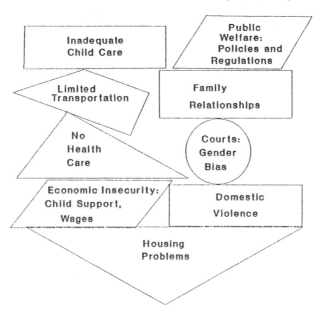

Second, their needs are not neatly piled in a hierarchical order that can be achieved in a linear fashion. Instead, a jumbled set of issues teeter like irregularly shaped building blocks that rarely seem to come together in a coordinated fashion and yet are interdependent elements (see Figure 1.1). Economic insecurity from low wages and unreliable child support payments, the high cost of quality child care, pressures of losing health insurance, and threats of eviction from an apartment for inability to pay increasing rents are just some of the stresses that foster family instability. The shape, size, and function of each building block are determined by private- and public-sector policies and interests as well as individual actions by family members and the mother herself.

This book suggests that the goal of family stability can be more readily attained for single-parent families if basic needs for shelter, food, and physical safety are conceived in a different way. There are levels of need that are interrelated and must be considered simultaneously (see Figure 1.2).

Level 1: Residential Stability. The first level consists of safe, affordable, habitable, and permanent housing. This ring becomes the cement for developing family stability. Shelter security requires diverse housing types in order to meet the variety of family situations and needs. For example,

Figure 1.2
Levels of Need in One-Parent Families: Family Stability

LEVELS OF NEED

1. RESIDENTIAL STABILITY -
   safe, affordable, habitable
   permanent housing

2. PERSONAL SAFETY -
   freedom from domestic
   violence; need for
   physically adequate
   shelter in safe
   neighborhoods

3. BELONGING, FAMILY
   RELATIONSHIPS -
   connection with
   others; quality
   parent-child relations

4. SELF-ESTEEM -
   self-worth, confidence
   in skills; ability to
   reenter education,
   training, employment

5. SELF-DISCOVERY, VISION -
   sense of control over
   one's life choices

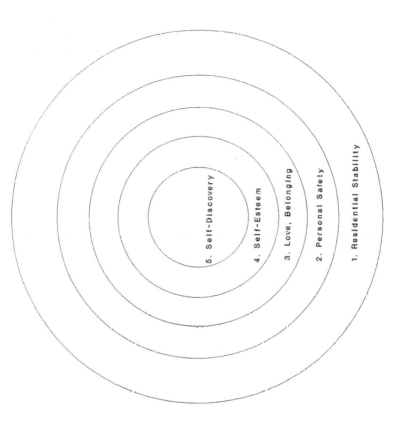

one-parent families may need to house-share or double up to make housing costs affordable. Some may need affordable apartments near suburban employment. Others may need temporary shelter in service-intensive group homes.

Level 2: Personal Safety. Personal safety and security are made possible when physically adequate shelter is located in safe neighborhoods that are free of violent crime. Freedom from domestic violence at this level involves the vigilance of community police and a reformed court system.

Level 3: Belonging, Family, Love Relationships. Breaking through the isolation and loneliness associated with the breakdown of marital relationships can eventually lead to new relationships if a single parent achieves the necessary stability and security provided by Levels 1 and 2. Once the family is residentially stable and safe, attention can be paid to the adjustment of internal family coping systems, such as new parenting relationships between a mother and her children. Then other personal connections, love, and feelings of belongingness can help a single parent develop a sense of confidence and self-worth that leads to independence.

Level 4: Self-Esteem. A sense of being valued by others which replaces feelings of worthlessness experienced by so many single mothers after a traumatic divorce and separation, especially when domestic violence was involved, stimulates their self-esteem. The self-confidence derived from this tier enables single mothers to gain the education necessary for new employment; enter technical or vocational training programs; make child care decisions and select qualified child care providers; assertively go back to court to enforce or modify child support orders or seek orders of protection in cases of domestic violence; conduct job searches; competitively enter the labor market and negotiate needed benefits plans and wage rates; solve dilemmas of sexual harassment at the workplace without leaving the job; and finally manage work/family tensions while still being a good parent.

Level 5: Self-Discovery, Vision. The process of developing oneself to the fullest potential is achievable in Level 5 where a sense of powerlessness over events in one's life is replaced with autonomy and control. At this level new knowledge and skills are acquired. The relationship with the children may seem closer. Accommodations and adjustments have been made with family and friends. Inventory of personal strengths as well as weakness has been taken. Expectations and life realities have been pondered: achievements at midlife, what marriage is and is not, aspirations for the future. Once expectations have been adjusted, and scaled back if necessary, a vision of the future can then emerge.

Basic Needs As Nested Circles

The most fundamental needs of shelter and safety are critical because they form the foundation on which other basic needs can then be met. Families who experience housing displacement and homelessness after relationship breakdown are most vulnerable to long-term fear for personal safety, isolation and loneliness, feelings of worthlessness, and, ultimately, powerlessness over their own life events. In contrast, those who have the greatest economic and housing security have stability from which to meet their needs for personal safety and security, belongingness, family and love relationships, self-esteem, and self-discovery.

In order to achieve stability, however, single mothers need to replace the haphazardly stacked blocks that currently represent elements of their lives. When one block is removed—be it a child care arrangement, transportation to work, or housing displacement—the entire structure collapses. The family may spend years trying to reassemble the stack of blocks.

Not only does the stack have a propensity to teeter, but also different blocks keep falling out. A single mother's situation is like the legendary person who puts a finger in the dike to hold back the rushing water, only to discover that more leaks keep developing, each requiring immediate and undivided attention. Such vigilance to survival tasks prevents any focus on higher level needs.

How do we reconcile these needs with the new economic realities? What are likely roles for local, state, and federal levels of government in responding to competing needs and interests? What are the respective roles for the private and nonprofit sectors? What is the individual responsibility of single parents themselves? A practical starting point for this process of stabilization moves beyond easy moralizing that blames and stigmatizes single mothers for their social and economic situations to a larger perspective that values stabilization of all family forms.

First, all five levels of need must be considered at the same time. Figure 1.2 depicts a holistic framework showing how these basic needs are nested in levels. Employment and training programs, for example, require the single parent to have self-esteem. This level of personal development is not possible unless the family's needs for residential stability, personal safety, and social connectedness are being met as well.

Second, an understanding of the interdependence among these levels of need requires knowledge about political, social, and economic forces that either facilitate or hinder the individual mother's ability to meet her own needs. Students of urban economics, geography, political science, sociology, urban planning, architecture, and other disciplines that investigate spatial and political impacts of large-scale economic change—including the changing structure of cities—should be acquainted with the social impacts of such changes on neighborhoods and households, especially where factors of gender, race, and class intersect.[5] Students of psychology, social work, and disciplines that examine the functioning and interaction of individuals and families should be acquainted with forces in the external environment, especially trends in federal housing policy, public- and private-sector urban development, and local-level land-use zoning that have profound impacts on individual behavior and family well-being.

FOCUS OF THE BOOK

This book is a primer on the quality of life, the life choices, and chances of single-mother families. The topic of single-mother families is relevant, important, and controversial. It has received widespread attention because of its nontraditional family structure; its socioeconomic status; societal interest in the welfare of its children; and implications for social welfare policy.

The unique contribution of this book is that it examines the wholeness of the single-parent experience that includes the social *and* physical environments, an integrative step not generally attempted in social science research. Several questions are posed. What are the sources of stresses, strengths, and needs from the perspective of single mothers themselves? The focus on relevant dimensions of a range of human needs necessitates an interdisciplinary approach in order to (1) better understand how environmental forces outside the family influence well-being inside the family unit, and (2) draw policy implications for family strengthening. Definitions of what we mean by the social and physical environments follow.

Social Environment

The social context, or environment, of the single parent refers to inter-actions among individuals and groups of individuals at two levels. The first consists of close relationships such as those with family, friends, peers, or intimate others; and community of common interests such as religious, ethnicity, or race. The second level consists of less personal relationships such as work organizations, schools, or other associations in which a person assumes a role as citizen, producer, consumer, or client.[6]

The social environment also refers to *social norms*—examples of which are values, traditions, life-styles, rules, obligations, regulations, and duties; *social institutions*—the economy, the family, the political order, and religion; and *institutional arrangements*—working agreements about the distribution of wealth, power, prestige, and privilege associated with race, ethnicity, gender, age, marital status, or sexual orientation. While designed to create stability for a society, institutional arrangements also are a source of conflict for those who experience institutional inequities.

Physical Environment

The physical environment refers to the "built" environment: the geographic or spatial organization of the metropolitan landscape; use of land and its resources; city structure; the design, location, and quality of living spaces such as neighborhoods; and the quality of housing. Because housing is a basic human need central to the raising of children, this book represents an approach to housing which is considerably broader than the traditional interests in overcrowding, physical deficiencies, and facilities. Housing concerns health, affordability, security and safety, neighborhood and social relations, status, community facilities and services, access to jobs, and control over environments.[7]

This particular approach was selected in order to bridge the gap between what academics often consider disparate fields of inquiry, yet what single parents experience as a seamless web of interactions. Researchers from a range of academic disciplines have examined the one-parent family but from different perspectives that include family functioning (or dysfunction) and appropriate therapeutic interventions; children's mental health; and educational and occupational attainment. Such books focus on the pattern of interrelationships among family members and ways to resolve problems internal to the family system. One-parent families are typically discussed in reference to deviant family forms, because they do not fit into conventional models of the life cycle.

Others investigate the impacts of divorce and child support, or address issues of unwed teen motherhood, urban poverty, and growth of the "underclass."[8] Such books are policy-based, focusing on social problems such as urban poverty, and investigate the implications of large-scale social policies such as public welfare and child support on single-parent economic well-being.

Between these two points on the continuum of family studies is the little-explored area of interactions between single mothers and individuals and groups representing various institutions in their environments: school teachers, landlords, police officers, employers, bankers, creditors, neighbors, welfare workers, family members, ex-husbands, lawyers, judges, real estate agents, and many others whose behavior influences their life choices.

Findings from studies based on quantitative analysis of large data sets help to define and better interpret the single-parent phenomenon. However, there is still a gap in what we know about this substantial segment of our population. For example, the federal Welfare Reform Act of 1988 that was implemented by states in 1993 has a welfare-to-work element with a goal of reducing poverty among single-mother families by transitioning them into waged work. But how much do we know about the exigencies single mothers face in getting and keeping a job? Single mothers face a tangle of factors that affect opportunities for good wages and higher income levels: the number and ages of children; availability of affordable child care; wage levels offered; location of their home, of child care, and of employment; work schedules; required education and job skills; benefits offered; stability of housing arrangements; and transportation. This book attempts to untangle these factors.

The Study

The idea for this book developed after publication of *Women As Single Parents: Confronting Institutional Barriers in the Courts, the Workplace, and the Housing Market* (1988), a book that initially outlined multiple barriers to low-income, single-parent family well-being and recommended greater interdisciplinary research.[9] The rationale was based on three concerns. First, while policy analysts were debating ways to decrease dependency on public welfare programs by requiring welfare recipients to work, this research indicated that most single mothers' lives were extraordinarily complex; their ability to work was intricately intertwined not only with child care concerns but also with housing issues. When low-income single mothers with housing subsidies made decisions to improve the quality of their lives through the same free-market housing choices used by middle- and upper-income families—the freedom to move—they were typically thwarted by institutional arrangements that kept them "in their place." The place for low-income black and Hispanic women meant being trapped and stuck in the densely populated, dilapidated, and unsafe urban neighborhoods they were trying to escape.

Second, the population of single parents is diverse, and questions emerged about the quality of life and life-chances of single mothers from a range of socioeconomic conditions. Third, in the last five years inner-city neighborhoods experienced increasing rates of physical deterioration and social dislocation, and the housing market was "softer"; housing prices had started to come down. The need for a new research project based on an interdisciplinary, multimethod approach was evident. Both micro-level analysis (on individual mothers) and macro-level analysis (on neighborhoods, events, policies) were indicated.

Micro-level data were collected in a qualitative study of seventy-three single mothers. It was a purposive sample intended to include diversity in demographic characteristics; in location of residence; and in housing tenure, that is, homeownership or renter status. A structured interview schedule was designed and used in personal interviews that were conducted, whenever possible, in the woman's own home. Some interviews were conducted in social service agencies, in homeless shelters, and in city parks in order to interview hard-to-locate and understudied populations of teen mothers and homeless women with school-aged children. Interviews were audio-recorded and transcribed for analysis. These methods geographically circumscribed the qualitative study to New England and primarily to eastern Massachusetts. The women range in age from 16 to 70 and represent the well-to-do, the middle-income, the working poor, and the very poor. Where women's stories are reported in subsequent chapters, their names and identifying information have been changed to protect their privacy.

Current U.S. Census Bureau and other government agency statistics and scholarly research reports were analyzed. Interviews were conducted with federal, state, and local officials who administer social welfare and affordable housing programs. Neighborhood-level analyses were performed by participant-observation methods in urban, suburban, and rural areas where respondents lived.

OVERVIEW

The focus on social and physical environments led to some surprising findings. Women were found to be on the "edge" or at the margins of the housing market and uprooted unless their own earnings permitted them to independently afford market-rate housing.

- Irregular, insufficient, or nonreceipt of child support created problems in maintaining housing stability.

- A pattern of frequent residential mobility emerged that affected the ability of single mothers to maintain consistent employment. This housing-employment link helped to put them on the "edge" of the labor market as well.

- An unanticipated theme of domestic violence emerged regardless of marital status, homeowner/renter status, age, race, or income. A woman's own home was an unsafe place for her to be. Those who experienced domestic violence were on the "edge" of personal safety and security.

The book is divided into three sections. Part I presents background information on one-parent families which establishes a foundation on which the remainder of the book rests. Transformational social and economic shifts are analyzed in Chapter 2. Demographic trends show diversity and a shift in family form during the past thirty years; the increase in one-parent families is only one of many of these trends. The impacts of economic restructuring are discussed relative to changing levels and sources of family economic support for women and men.

Chapter 3 provides a theoretical background on trends in the physical environment—especially urban housing and neighborhood environments—that are important to one-parent families. This chapter explores the fundamental concepts in urban restructuring that focus on the decline of urban America and the emergence of urban instability for inner-city families. Four questions are posed: What happened to America's cities? How does the housing market work? How are housing and employment issues related to single-parent families? What are the race, class, and gender implications of housing segregation? The chapter concludes that social dislocation for left-behind families is a result of urban neighborhood instability fostered in large measure by public and private decisions regarding zoning and land-use policies, tax code enforcement, public housing strategies, and real estate practices. Finally, dimensions of homelessness are explained that include an examination of the structural and personal context of this housing problem.

Part II introduces findings from the qualitative study of single mothers. This section examines how single mothers attempt to meet their three most basic needs: personal safety from a violent relationship with an ex-husband or partner, an affordable housing unit, and a job with benefits that pay a living wage.

Chapter 4 examines the role of domestic violence in relationship breakdown and women's search for the most basic of needs—personal safety. Which social institutions and social arrangements help battered women locate safe housing, and which hinder it? The chapter considers the influence of increasing violence in American culture and the escalation of drugs, gangs, and domestic violence in the nation's larger cities on family well-being.

Chapter 5 examines the role of women in the workforce. Three questions are posed: Can women support families on their wages alone? What barriers to employment do they encounter, and how are the barriers overcome? How does the location of their housing affect employment prospects and family stability? A high cost of working emerged as a clear theme among single-parent mothers. High costs refer to a multiplicity of barriers to employment in the face of low-wage expectations for the jobs most women perform.

Housing and neighborhood needs are addressed in chapters 6 and 7. Chapter 6 examines the housing needs of teen mothers in urban poverty. Their housing needs for affordable rental units in safe neighborhoods are identified, and their frustrations and coping strategies in trying to secure public, subsidized, and private rental housing—as well as education—are examined. The chapter points out key roles played by the teen's family of origin, father of the baby, individual actions and responsibilities of young mothers themselves, and housing policies and regulations.

The role of housing in divorce is explored in Chapter 7. A theme of being displaced or uprooted was observed in the separated and divorced who had marital housing. Which forces help to create housing displacement, and which forces mediate it? This chapter highlights the day-to-day housing problems of affordability and of location for separated and divorced single parents. It illustrates how the key housing and urban policy dilemmas identified in Chapter 3 affect suburban single mothers in the reality of their everyday existence.

Part III focuses on the transition toward a more stable family situation at two levels. Chapter 8 presents examples of how women restructure their lives in the aftermath of divorce. The chapter discusses how divorced women have a more difficult time transitioning to family stability than do widows or the never-married, but that stability is possible when family and community-based support systems are available and utilized.

Chapter 9, the concluding chapter, examines what public institutions can do, especially through housing and community development initiatives, to strengthen family life in ways that benefit one-parent families. Actions directed at both private industry and local, state, and federal government are suggested. Specific recommendations are made to redirect a vision and public actions toward a caring society in which humane cities function as if *all* children and families mattered.

Excluded from this book is a detailed discussion of health care, personal adjustment, and public welfare reform. These issues are addressed by others. Our purpose here is to fill a gap in understanding how basic needs that are not usually addressed in a connected way—housing and residential stability, economic security, and personal safety—are in fact linked in very important ways that are necessary to ensure family stability.

NOTES

1. U.S. Senate confirmation hearing of Judge Ruth Bader Ginsburg, July 20–24, 1993.

2. U.S. Department of Labor, Bureau of Labor Statistics, "Employment in Perspective: Women in the Labor Force," Report 822, Fourth Quarter (Washington, D.C.: U.S. Government Printing Office, 1991).

3. U.S. Bureau of the Census, "Money Income of Households, Families, and Persons in the United States: 1990," *Current Population Reports*, Series P-60, No. 176 (Washington, D.C.: U.S. Government Printing Office, 1992), Table 13.

4. William W. Goldsmith and Edward Blakely, *Separate Societies: Poverty and Inequality in U.S. Cities* (Philadelphia: Temple University Press, 1992).

5. M. Gottdiener and Chris G. Pickvance, eds., *Urban Life in Transition, Urban Affairs Annual Reviews* 39 (Newbury Park, Calif.: Sage Publications, 1991), p. 4.

6. John Longres, *Human Behavior in the Social Environment* (Itasca, Ill.: Peacock Publishers, 1990).

7. Jon Pynoos, Robert Schafer, and Chester Hartman eds., *Housing Urban America*, 2nd ed. (New York: Aldine Publishing, 1980), p. 1.

8. See, for example, Monica McGoldrick and Betty Carter, eds., *The Changing Family Life Cycle* (Boston: Allyn and Bacon, 1989); G. Duncan and W. Rodgers, "Single-Parent Families: Are Their Economic Problems Transitory or Persistent?" *Family Planning Perspectives* 19, No. 4 *(1987)*: 171–178; Christopher Jencks, "Is the American Underclass Growing?" in *The Urban Underclass*, C. Jencks and P. Peterson, eds., (Washington, D.C.: Brookings Institution, 1991), p. 84; Charles Murray, *Losing Ground* (New York: Basic Books, 1984); William Julius Wilson, *The Truly Disadvantaged: The Inner City, the Underclass, and Public Policy* (Chicago: University of Chicago Press, 1987); Mary Jo Bane and David Ellwood, *Single Mothers and Their Living Arrangements,* Report prepared for the Department of Health and Human Services, Cambridge, Mass.: Harvard University, 1984, mimeo; Irwin Garfinkel and Sara McLanahan, *Single Mothers and Their Children* (Washington, D.C.: Urban Institute Press, 1986); Sheldon H. Danzinger and Daniel H. Weinburg, eds., *Fighting Poverty* (Cambridge, Mass.: Harvard University Press, 1986); Lenore Weitzman, *The Divorce Revolution: The Unexpected Social and Economic Consequences for Women and Children in*

America (New York: Free Press, 1985); Heather Ross and Isabel Sawhill, *Time of Transition: The Growth of Families Headed by Women* (Washington, D.C.: Urban Institute, 1975); and David Ellwood, "The Changing Structure of American Families," *Journal of the American Planning Association* 59, No. 1 (Winter 1993): 3–8.

9. Elizabeth A. Mulroy, "The Search for Affordable Housing," in *Women As Single Parents: Confronting Institutional Barriers in the Courts, the Workplace, and the Housing Market*, ed. Elizabeth A. Mulroy (Dover, Mass.: Auburn House Publishing Co., 1988), pp. 123–163.

—2—

Thirty Years of Family and Workplace Change

The increase in the number of one-parent families marks a dramatic change, but it is only one of many challenging changes that has diversified household composition in the 1990s. The breadwinner-homemaker model that characterized "the family" in the 1950s has been replaced by a multitude of family forms—stepfamilies, single parents, extended and multigenerational families, unmarried couples, families that "double up" to make ends meet, and subfamilies that live in the households of others. In addition, marriage rates are falling, divorce rates are rising, and young people are postponing or foregoing marriage altogether.

Our objective is to establish, in general terms, the significance of single-parent families. In order to do this, we must understand the demographic makeup of this population—its racial makeup, marital status, sex, age, educational levels, participation in the workforce, employability, and levels of income. This chapter examines (1) changes in the demography of families during the past thirty years and (2) changes in family economic support, including the impacts of structural changes on work and employment. Far-reaching demographic change is not limited to the United States. Low marriage and low fertility rates, high divorce rates, and high rates of births outside of marriage are seen in many other industrialized nations. The focus is on the United States, but occasional comparison will be made with other countries. This offers a perspective on whether the significant changes affecting the family are peculiar to the United States or whether they are also affecting other societies.

DEMOGRAPHIC CHANGES

The United States Census Bureau distinguishes between a household and a family:

- **Families**—Two or more persons related by birth, marriage, or adoption who reside together.
- **Households**—All persons who occupy a particular dwelling unit such as a house, an apartment, or a condominium intended for living quarters. A household may consist of one person who lives alone or a group that shares a housing unit.

Under this definition, all families form households, but not all households are families. The distinction is referred to as *family* households and *nonfamily* households. Recent data from the U.S. Census Bureau distinguish seven key family trends:

- Changes in household composition
- Postponement of marriage
- Increase in cohabitation
- Increase in divorce
- Decrease in childbirth inside of marriage
- Increase in childbirth outside of marriage
- Increase in one-parent families

Household Composition

Over the past twenty years, family households have declined, while nonfamily households have increased. One of the most dramatic trends observed in American family life is the decline in total married couple families from 70.6 percent of all households in 1970 to 56.1 in 1990. In addition, married couples with children declined from 40.3 percent in 1970 to only 26.3 in 1990, while "other family" and nonfamily households increased. Nonfamily households in particular increased from 18.8 percent to 29.2 percent from 1970 to 1990 (see Figure 2.1).

Nonfamily households are a diverse population. In fact, from 1940 to 1990 the number of nonfamily households in which persons were not related by blood, birth, marriage, adoption, or other legal arrangement increased tenfold. This household category includes (1) young people who can afford the cost of housing on one income and choose to live alone, and (2) the elderly, who comprise an increasing proportion of the population because

Figure 2.1
Household Composition: 1970 to 1990 (Percent)

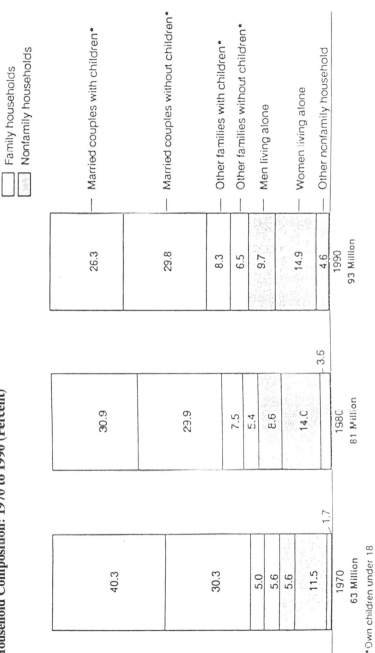

Family households
Nonfamily households

	1970 63 Million	1980 81 Million	1990 93 Million	
Married couples with children*	40.3	30.9	26.3	
Married couples without children*	30.3	23.9	29.8	
Other families with children*	5.0	7.5	8.3	
Other families without children*	5.6	5.4	6.5	
Men living alone	5.6	8.6	9.7	
Women living alone	11.5	14.0	14.9	
Other nonfamily household	1.7	3.6	4.6	

*Own children under 18

Source: U.S. Bureau of the Census, "Household and Family Characteristics: March 1990 and 1989," *Current Population Reports*, Series P-20, No. 447 (Washington, D.C.: U.S. Government Printing Office, 1990), p. 2.

of improved medical care and the availability of elderly public and subsidized housing that enables more of them to afford to live alone.

Other nonfamily households include cohabitating couples and groups of adults who share an apartment or a house. This category nearly tripled from 1.7 percent in 1970 to 4.6 percent in 1990.

Postponing Marriage

Americans have always had one of the highest marriage rates in the world. However, the proportion of men and women in their twenties and thirties who have never married has grown rapidly:

- In 1990, only half as many young adults ages 18 to 24 maintained their own families as did in 1960.
- During the last twenty years, the proportion of never-married persons 30 to 34 years old nearly tripled.
- Those who do marry are now older. The median age at first marriage increased from a low of 20 years for women and 22 years for men in 1950 to 23 years for women and 26 years for men in 1990. This trend is similar to marital age patterns that existed at the turn of the last century.

Increase in Cohabitation

For many young adults, as well as older single and divorced adults, cohabitation offers an increasingly popular living arrangement. The United States has historically maintained a rather low level of nonmarital cohabitation (under 3 percent), unlike its European counterparts where unmarried couples living together is common. In the United States, the trends are changing.

In 1990, there were 2.9 million unmarried-couple households in America, a sixfold increase in twenty years. The largest proportion were never-married men and women ages 25 to 34 years. About one-third of these households had children under 15 years of age living with them who were biological offspring of the cohabitating partners, as well as children of a divorced parent now living with a new partner.[1]

Decrease in Childbirth Inside of Marriage

A decrease in childbirth inside of marriage has reduced the size of American families. Several different patterns of behavior account for this trend. First, the fertility rates of women have fluctuated over time. At the turn of the century, it was common for women to bear about seven children, but the number dropped to 2.1 by the mid-1930s. The post–World War II baby boom sent fertility rates up to 3.7 births per woman, but then in the mid-1970s rates tumbled down to 1.8—less than the necessary replacement level of 2.1 children per woman. Black women never fell below the replacement level, although fertility rates for black and white women show similar time-line patterns.

The timing of births is, in part, responsible for decreasing family size. Increasing age at first marriage and increasing educational attainment of women delay entry into motherhood and influence decisions to remain childless.[2]

Increase in Childbirth Outside of Marriage

Births to unmarried women of all ages increased from 224,000 in 1960 to over one million in 1989—nearly a fivefold increase in three decades. By 1989:

- After two decades of declining birthrates to women under 20, a sharp upswing in births to teens occurred. The birthrate for young women ages 15 to 17 rose 19 percent in just three years from 1986 to 1989. However, more than two-thirds of all births outside of marriage were still to women over 20.
- Two of every three black infants, one of every three Hispanic infants, and one of every five white infants were born to unmarried mothers.
- An increasing share of older, never-married white women made the deliberate choice to bear a child.[3]

Although some observers are concerned about the high percentage of births to women outside of marriage in the United States, it is similar to percentages in Canada, France, the United Kingdom, and other industrialized countries. In Sweden, childbirth outside of marriage is twice as high as in the United States. In contrast, nonmarital childbearing in Japan is extremely low at 1 percent of all births.[4]

Teens, like other age groups, are delaying marriage even if they become pregnant. Today, over 60 percent of all births to teens occur outside of marriage—almost three times the rate of the early 1960s.

Only a small portion of unmarried childbearing occurs by choice. Two-thirds of never-married mothers reported that their pregnancy was unintended (that is, either mistimed or unwanted), compared with about one-third of married women. Such feelings at conception do not mean that the child, once born, is unloved or uncared for. Mothers and fathers who did not plan the pregnancy may want and love the child who is born. One in four births outside of marriage are to two-parent—though unmarried—households.[5]

Increase in Divorce

In 1990 there were 2.4 million marriages and 1.2 million divorces. Compared with the 1960s, the number of divorces and the divorce rate have more than doubled. The U.S. divorce rate is now the highest in the developed countries, twice that of Sweden, Denmark, Canada, and the United Kingdom.[6]

- Divorce is the most common path to singleness for young and middle-aged adults, while death of spouse is the most common path to singleness among the elderly.
- In 1990, 8 percent of the total U.S. adult population was divorced and not remarried. The number is higher for women than for men because women are less likely to remarry.
- If current divorce levels persist, approximately 50 percent of all recent marriages will eventually end in divorce.[7]

Divorce statistics do not include information on marital separation or the breakup of families in which the couple is not legally married. They therefore understate the extent of family breakup in all countries.

Increase in One-Parent Families

The U.S. Census Bureau began documenting one-parent families when their numbers increased dramatically in the 1970s, and because their socioeconomic profile is different from that of two-parent families. The Census Bureau uses the term *family group* to count those single parents who live independently as heads of households and also those who are *subfamilies* living in households of related or unrelated people. Most single parents maintain their own household; that is, they own or rent the living quarters in which they and their children reside, while 22 percent of single parents live in the households of others. The Census Bureau refers to these arrangements as a *family group. Single* is used throughout the book to include *all* those who parent alone; they may be divorced, separated, widowed, or never-married.

Size. By 1991, there were 10.1 million single-parent family groups in the United States (including both female- and male-headed families), up from 3.8 million in 1970 (see Figure 2.2). A dramatic increase is reflected in its proportion of all families with children. By 1991, 28.9 percent of all families with children were single-parent families, more than double the 13 percent in 1970.

Race. Two-thirds of all single-parent families are white; however, one-parent family situations are more prevalent among blacks and Hispanics. In 1991, 23 percent of white families with children under age 18 were headed by a single parent, compared with 62.6 percent of black families, and 33.1 percent of Hispanic families (see Figure 2.3).[8]

While diversity in family form can be observed among all races, it is most dramatic among black families. A precipitous decline in marriage, an increase in divorce, and to a lesser extent an increase in births outside of marriage among blacks has taken place. By 1990, only 50 percent of all black families were married-couple families, down more than two-thirds from 1970.[9]

Marital Status, Sex, and Age. Mothers head the vast majority of one-parent families. There were an estimated 8.7 million one-parent families maintained by mothers in 1991, representing 86.5 percent of all one-parent family situations (see Figure 2.4). Pathways to single parenthood include (1) marital separation, (2) divorce, (3) widowhood, and (4) births outside of marriage.

In 1991, divorced and separated mothers accounted for half (50.9 percent) of all one-parent families, whereas widows represented only 4.9 percent, a decline from 18 percent in 1970. The never-married category now represents 30.7 percent of all one-parent families. However, stark differences can be observed by race. Although births outside of marriage have increased among all races in the past twenty years, single-parent blacks and Hispanics are more likely to be never-married than whites, who are most likely to be divorced.[10]

The proportion of single fathers maintaining families is increasing. Single fathers accounted for 13.5 percent of one-parent families in 1991, up from 10.3 percent in 1970. The incidence of single fatherhood is higher among whites than blacks. Such fathers are most apt to be separated or divorced.

Single parents tend to be younger than married parents, and single mothers are younger than single fathers. The median age of single parents

Figure 2.2
Numbers: Trends in One-Parent Family Groups

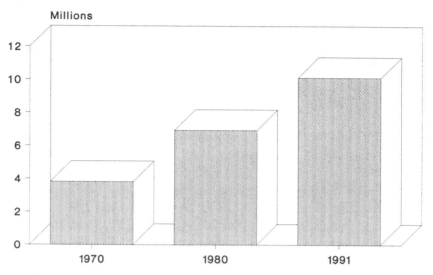

Millions

1970   1980   1991

Source: Adapted from U.S. Bureau of the Census, "Household and Family Characteristics,
Feb. 1992," *Current Population Reports,* P-20, No. 458, Table H.

is 32.7 years for single mothers and 36.5 years for single fathers. In contrast,
the median age for two-parent families is 37.4 years. Age differences have
implications for living arrangements, housing stability, and employability.
The younger a mother is when her first child is born, the more resources
she will need for economic viability and the more likely she will be to have
more children.

Educational Level of Parents. A parent's educational level is an important
factor in determining a child's level of socioeconomic well-being.[11] Children in one-parent families are twice as likely to live with a parent who has
not completed high school than are children in two-parent families.[12] In
1990, the proportion of children living with one parent who had not
completed high school was 30.1 percent, versus 16.1 percent of children in
two-parent families (see Figure 2.5).

The contrasts between children living in one- and two-parent families
are not as dramatic when the educational achievement of the parents was
high school or some college. However, children in two-parent families were
three times more likely to live in families where at least one parent had
graduated from a four-year college than were children in one-parent families.

Figure 2.3
Race: Family Groups with Children Under 18

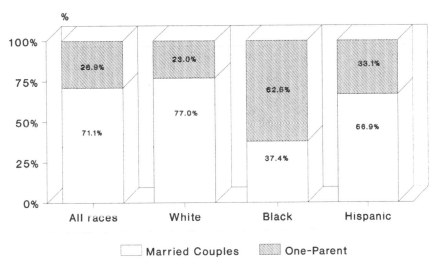

Source: Adapted from U.S. Bureau of the Census, "Household and Family Characteristics, Feb. 1992," *Current Population Reports*, P-20, No. 458, Table F.

Labor Force Status. Changing family structures during the past three decades are evident in trends of labor force statistics between one- and two-parent families. First, statistics on single parents show consistent and increasing participation in the labor force. This in itself could be an expected trend because this group of single parents relies only on themselves for long-term economic stability. In 1990, for example, 78 percent of all male-headed, one-parent families, and 62.7 percent of female-headed, one-parent families were in the labor force, up from 73 percent for fathers and 49.9 percent for mothers in 1960 (see Figure 2.6). This may reflect high motivation to provide a stable family environment through labor force participation, a difficult objective in our current economic climate.

The greatest pattern of change is in married-couple families. In 1990:

- More than half (53.5 percent) were dual-earner families with both wife and husband in the labor force, double the number in 1960 (see Figure 2.6).
- Only 25 percent were composed of a breadwinner father and stay-at-home mother, down from 60.7 percent in 1960.
- Only 8 percent were composed of a breadwinner mother and stay-at-home father.
- 17 percent had neither parent in the labor force.[13]

Figure 2.4
Marital Status of One-Parent Families

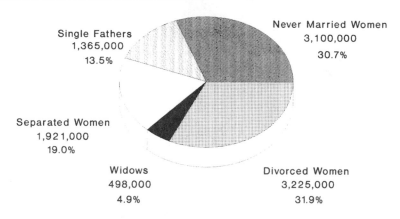

Source: Adapted from U.S. Bureau of the Census, "Household and Family Characteristics, Feb. 1992," *Current Population Reports*, P-20, No. 458, Table H.

These patterns have had a significant impact on role changes within two-parent families. Fathers and older children have assumed more responsibility for child care and homemaking while mothers have assumed breadwinner roles. Some mothers were the sole breadwinners in families with unemployed fathers, while others assumed co-breadwinner roles.[14]

Employment and Unemployment. A single parent's participation in the labor force is affected by several factors including educational level and the ages of children. Even with sole responsibility for family earnings and caregiving, more single mothers were in the workforce than women in dual-earner families.[15] In 1991, 58.8 percent of single mothers with children under the age of 6 and 77.9 percent of single mothers with children between 6 and 17 were in the labor force (see Figure 2.7). Moreover, their unemployment rate was twice that of married women in the workforce (9.1 percent compared to 4.5 percent).[16]

Income. Despite the high employment rate of single parents, these families are very likely to be struggling to get by. In single-parent families, 13.5 million children (86 percent) were living with their mothers. The family average (mean) income was $13,100, only half of the $26,000 earned by single-father families and only one-third of the $41,300 income of two-parent families with children. These disparities reflect the greater earning power of single fathers and the fact that two-parent families often have incomes of two working parents.[17]

Figure 2.5
Education: 1990, Single Parents with Children Under 18

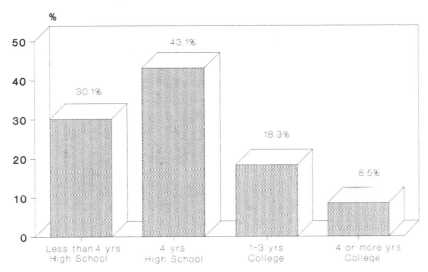

Source: Adapted from U.S. Bureau of the Census, "Marital Status and Living Arrangements: March 1990," *Current Population Reports,* P-20, No. 450.

The mean annual income for white single mothers was $14,900, $10,300 for blacks, and $10,100 for Hispanics. These income levels of female-headed families with children are at or below the U.S. government's poverty line. As a group, such families are a unit of social concern.

Poverty. The federal government's definition of the poverty rate is based on cash money income thresholds, which vary with family size and composition and do not take into account noncash benefits. In 1989, the poverty threshold for a family of four was $12,675. A four-person family with cash income less than this amount would be considered poor.

The increase in the number of single-parent families is not responsible for the rising poverty rates. While two incomes are clearly better than one, the poor tend to be poor before, during, and after they marry. The two-parent household is the fastest growing poverty group in the United States. The majority of the poor live in households with workers who are employed full-year and full-time. Sixty-four percent of all poor children live in families with one or more workers. Working full-time at minimum wage today still leaves a three-person family $2,300 below the poverty line.

Single mothers on public welfare (Aid to Families with Dependent Children—AFDC) have lower incomes than single mothers who work. The

Figure 2.6
Families and Labor Force Status

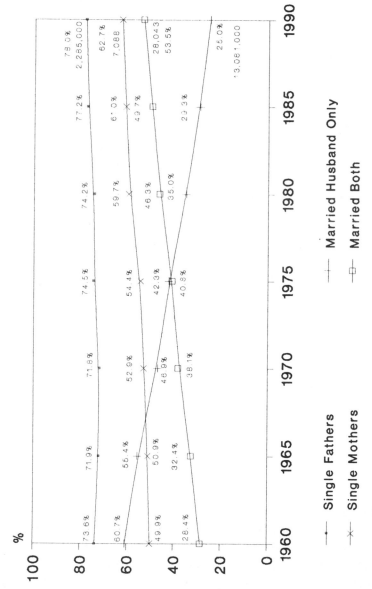

Source: Adapted from U.S. Dept. of Labor, Bureau of Labor Statistics, "Employment in Perspective: Women in the Labor Force," No. 822, Table A-17, p. 49.

Figure 2.7
Employment of Single Mothers with Children

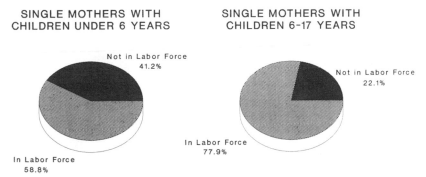

SINGLE MOTHERS WITH
CHILDREN UNDER 6 YEARS

SINGLE MOTHERS WITH
CHILDREN 6-17 YEARS

Not in Labor Force
41.2%

Not in Labor Force
22.1%

In Labor Force
77.9%

In Labor Force
58.8%

Source: Adapted from U.S. Dept of Labor, Bureau of Labor Statistics, "Employment in
Perspective: Women in the Labor Force, 1991," No. 822, Table A-18.

average welfare benefit in the United States is $367 a month, or $4,400 a
year. This is almost $9,000 less than the federal poverty line for a family of
three. In no state does the combination of welfare benefits and food stamps
together lift a family out of poverty.

Cross-national studies show that U.S. income support programs lifted
less than 5 percent of single mothers with children out of poverty in the
1980s, compared to 89 percent in the Netherlands, 81 percent in Sweden,
75 percent in the United Kingdom, 50 percent in France, 33 percent in
Germany, and 18.3 percent in Canada.[18]

The preceding text briefly outlines the characteristics of single-parent
family groups with children under age 18. The data show that single mothers
are working and are still poor. How do we reconcile their labor force
participation and their low incomes? The answer lies in the nature of the
jobs they perform. Single mothers most frequently work in blue-collar jobs
that offer low pay, few if any benefits, unstable employment, and few
opportunities for advancement. This is a type of discrimination called
occupational segregation and merits attention as a critical factor in single
mothers' work environments.

CHANGING TRENDS IN FAMILY ECONOMIC SUPPORT

Occupational Segregation

As a result of the occupational segregation, the overwhelming majority
of single mothers who work continue to do "women's work." Department

Figure 2.8
Family Income: Parents with Children Under 18

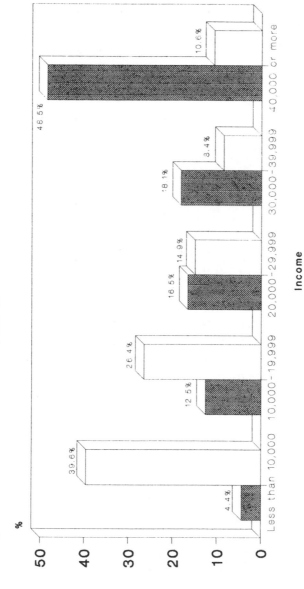

Source: Adapted from U.S. Bureau of the Census, "Marital Status and Living Arrangements: March 1990," *Current Population Reports*, P-20, No. 450.

of Labor statistics show that single mothers are distributed across all occupations, much as female workers in general are, with some exceptions:

- Single mothers are more likely to be service providers.
- They are less likely to be found in white-collar jobs.
- They are underrepresented in the typically female professions of nursing and teaching.
- They are more likely to have blue-collar jobs.

The Secondary Labor Market

Many single mothers work in the secondary labor market. This sector offers low wages, few or no benefits, and unstable employment. Work is often part-time, seasonal, or temporary. Workers receive few rewards for education or years on the job. Examples of secondary labor market jobs include domestic service, waiting on tables, farm work, or fast-food counter jobs. The "pink-collar ghetto" of women's service, manufacturing, and clerical work is generally considered part of the secondary sector. By contrast, the primary sector traditionally offers high wages, steady employment, and career ladders.

Historically, men had greater access to primary sector jobs that provided them with family wages to support home-bound women and children and brought some upward mobility over the course of their work lives.

Sex and race discrimination, gender roles, and lack of access to education confined the vast majority of white women and minority men and women to low-paying, secondary jobs. This occupational segregation kept minority and white women's earnings far below those of white men. Confinement to the secondary sector also creates higher risks of unemployment, explaining the fact that single mothers experience unemployment rates twice as high as those for all female workers.[19]

When differences in occupational distributions are examined by race, broad diversity can be seen. For example, white women are more than twice as likely to be found in white-collar occupations as black and Hispanic women, who are far more likely to be service providers. The black and Hispanic overrepresentation in service occupations extends across the range of high-paying service jobs such as fire and police and low-paying jobs such as domestic work. Black and Hispanic women are two to three times as likely as white women to be domestic servants.

Black and Hispanic women are overrepresented in blue-collar positions as well. They are four to five times as likely to be in construction as white women, even though such jobs employ only a tiny group of single mothers of any race. Black and Hispanic women are also more likely to be machine operators and assemblers than white women.[20] Women and men are affected by economic restructuring. This large-scale economic change has implications for family formation, of which one-parent families are a part.

Economic Restructuring

Economic support for the family has traditionally been based on men's labor force participation and income. The traditional family form assumed the presence of a male breadwinner whose income was sufficient to provide for a family's basic needs for housing (including homeownership), food, clothing, education of the children, and recreation. However, the global economy, a restructured workplace, and a labor market demand for better educated and highly skilled workers have drastically altered men's ability to be solo breadwinners. The restructured workplace is dividing workers into two tiers—the unskilled, underpaid, or unemployed group and the other a technologically well-paid elite.

The shift from an industrial to a service economy has resulted in a significant social change and a decline in jobs predominantly held by men:

- In 1987, 28 percent of all jobs were blue-collar jobs, down from 37 percent in 1960. Over 80 percent of these jobs were held by men.
- Since 1970, the greatest employment opportunities have shifted to low-wage, service-sector jobs that favors women.[21]
- Older mill-based and smokestack manufacturing industries were replaced with positions at average salaries only 68 percent as high.

In 1988, only 75 percent of men participated in the labor force, down from 83 percent in 1960. The decline was the most pronounced among married men, who typically have the highest labor force participation.[22] This decline reflects the aging of the population, with older, married men leaving the workplace, and the declining employability of young men with low educational attainment.

Education. Skill requirements are escalating throughout the economy. The U.S. Department of Labor has documented that the more years of schooling a man has the longer his worklife expectancy.[23]

- Over the last two decades, the employment rates of young men aged 16 to 24 with less than a high school education have declined from 87 to 83 percent.

- Of men aged 45 to 64 with less than a high school education, only 63 percent are employed.

Trends like these suggest that men with less than a high school education will have more difficulty gaining employment. A review of high school completion statistics yields confusing results. On the positive side, more blacks are graduating from high school—81 percent in 1986, up from 72 percent in 1976. However, a serious educational failure continues in big-city high schools where dropout rates of 40 to 50 percent by black, Hispanic, and Asian teenagers are reported. At the college level, the trend continues. In 1970, nearly 30 percent of black high school graduates 18 to 24 years old were enrolled in college. By 1988, that percentage had slipped to 25 percent.[24]

There is growing global competitive pressure for a highly skilled work-force, and the United States is facing a tremendous mismatch between the jobs available and the ability of Americans to perform them. An underedu-cated workforce that cannot keep pace with skill requirements will lose those jobs to international labor that meets the more knowledge-intensive work requirements. In Japan, 90 percent of teenagers complete high school. Their school year is longer, and their curriculum is considered more rigorous; some argue that an average high school education in Japan can be equated with an average college education in America.[25]

Job Loss. Plant closings across the country in the 1980s resulted in millions of American workers losing their jobs. Between January 1981 and January 1990, the Bureau of Labor Statistics reported that 11.7 million American workers were laid off. One-third remained unemployed or left the workforce. Of the two-thirds reemployed, many who previously held skilled manufacturing jobs had to take service-sector jobs at drastically reduced wages.[26]

Income Decline. Current economic trends have precipitated a sharp decline in men's earning capacity. In the mid-1960s, about one-fourth of all white men and 42 percent of all black men aged 24 to 34 had income below the poverty level for a family of four. By 1987, the number of those below the poverty level had increased substantially. Only one-third of white men but over half of black men had an income inadequate to support a family.[27]

Reversal in income growth happened suddenly. Between 1955 and 1973, the median income of men grew substantially—from $15,056 to $24,621. Then growth stopped. Earnings, adjusted for inflation, started to fall, and by 1987 the male wage was down to $19,859, a drop of 19 percent.[28] From 1979 to 1989—the decade of economic expansion and opportunity for many—black wage earners experienced an income drop of $1,330 in median earnings, while white males experienced a drop of $1,230.[29]

Prior to 1973, families could count on a steady growth of income from the male head of household as job advancement occurred and the economy grew. After 1973, women flooded the labor market to shore up family income. Dual-earner families in service-sector jobs are now working harder to earn the same income as one wage earner brought home from a well-paid smokestack manufacturing job twenty years ago.[30]

Such trends as men's declining educational attainment, reduced labor force participation, and declining incomes are problematic not only for the nation's ability to supply skilled and knowledgeable workers to meet workforce demands, but also for young women who seek male partners capable of providing stable family economic support into the twenty-first century. This is particularly true for young black adults. The trends suggest that young black women, for example, have little to gain financially from marrying young black men at this time. Remaining single improves their opportunities for greater educational attainment and reduces the risk of pregnancy.

Workplace Insecurity: The High-Tech Example. The impacts of economic restructuring affect white-collar as well as blue-collar employment, causing insecurity in the workplace for both men and women managers and men and women on the factory floor. In high technology, as one industry example, the prolonged economic recession has caused large and small industries to respond in three ways.

First, fundamental structural changes were implemented in the workplace that organize workers by cross-functional teams of generalists, away from the formerly specialized corporate divisions. This affects the content of jobs, who is hired, and who is fired. No one is immune. Blue-collar factory workers, white-collar middle managers, scientists, and engineers, pink-collar secretaries, and gray-collar technicians are all affected by the way work has been restructured to increase productivity.

Second, the slow economy prompted companies to seek ways to reduce outlays for benefits programs—health insurance, pension plans, and wage compensation benefits. They did so by cutting the ranks of permanent, full-time employees and replacing them with part-timers, subcontractors, consultants, and temporary workers to whom they pay no benefits. This is occurring throughout entire companies from secretarial levels to accountants, scientists, and engineers.

Third, high-tech information systems companies are hiring people from overseas. Not only do global telecommunications make a worker's geographic location irrelevant, but also many foreign workers are educated and trained professionals who will work for less money than their American counterparts.[31]

To the extent that these trends are observed across many industries, such hard economic realities portend serious problems for family economic stability in the next five years. Structural changes in the workplace mean that there will be:

- A growing gap between high- and low-wage workers.

- Fewer permanent position jobs and more part-time positions.

- More competition for all jobs, especially for the lower-skilled, service-sector jobs between highly trained laid-off workers, the less educated workers, and new trainees.

- Greater global competition for available jobs because of a preponderance of telecommunication systems and the ease of work relocation offshore.

- Reluctance among downsized companies to implement worker protection laws such as the Family and Medical Leave Act of 1993 and potential universal health insurance legislation, thereby reducing the number of permanent positions and shifting to part-time positions without benefits.

Reliance on a source other than the workplace for benefits packages will be required.

SUMMARY

The family as an institution has changed so much in the past thirty years that individual family members, employers, and government policymakers are hard-pressed to respond to the new fluid family patterns. The increase in one-parent families can be seen as one of many profound changes in family form taking place around the world. There are several underlying reasons for this pattern of family change; social, cultural, and economic factors have all played a role. As we focus on meeting family needs—and significant structural changes are central—family members, whether married, single parents, or sharing households, will need more intensive educational preparation for competitive jobs, a living wage, and supportive family and community systems so that basic needs can be met in new and different ways in the uncertain decade of the 1990s.

NOTES

1. U.S. Bureau of the Census, "Marital Status and Living Arrangements: March 1990," *Current Population Reports*, Series P-20, No. 450 (Washington, D.C.: U.S. Government Printing Office, 1991), p. 15.

2. Dennis A. Ahlburg and Carol J. DeVita, "New Realities of the American Family," *Population Bulletin*, 47, No. 2 (Washington, D.C.: Population Reference Bureau, August 1992), p. 18.

3. Ibid.

4. Ibid., pp. 22–23.

5. Ibid., p. 23.

6. C. Sorrentino, "The Changing Family in International Perspective," *Monthly Labor Review* 113, No. 3 (March 1990): 44.

7. Arlene Saluter, "Singleness in America," U.S. Bureau of the Census, "Studies in Marriage and the Family," *Current Population Reports*, Series P-23, No. 163 (Washington, D.C.: U.S. Government Printing Office, 1989), p. 4.

8. Steve Rawlings, "Single Parents and Their Children," U.S. Bureau of the Census, "Studies in Marriage and the Family," *Current Population Reports*, Series P-23, No. 162 (Washington, D.C.: U.S. Government Printing Office, 1989), Table B, p. 14.

9. U.S. Bureau of the Census, "Household and Family Characteristics: March 1990 and 1989," *Current Population Reports*, Series P-20, No. 447 (Washington, D.C.: U.S. Government Printing Office, 1990), Figure 3, p. 6.

10. Rawlings, "Single Parents and Their Children," Table C, p. 16.

11. Ibid., p. 21.

12. U.S. Bureau of the Census, "Marital Status and Living Arrangements," Figure 6.

13. U.S. Department of Labor, Bureau of Labor Statistics, "Employment in Perspective: Women in the Labor Force," Report 822, Fourth Quarter (Washington, D.C.: U.S. Government Printing Office, 1991), p. 33.

14. Ibid., Table A-17, p. 49.

15. Ibid.

16. Ibid., Table 1, p. 3.

17. U.S. Bureau of the Census, "Money Income of Households, Families, and Persons in the United States: 1990," *Current Population Reports*, Series P-60, No. 174 (Washington, D.C.: U.S. Government Printing Office, 1991), Table 13.

18. See Mimi Abramovitz and Fred Newdom, *Bertha Capen Reynolds Society Newsletter,* 4, No.3 (Spring 1992).

19. U.S. Department of Labor, Bureau of Labor Statistics, "Employment in Perspective," Table 1, p. 3.

20. Teresa Amott, "Working for Less: Single Mothers in the Workplace," in *Women As Single Parents: Confronting Institutional Barriers in the Courts, the Workplace, and the Housing Market*, ed. Elizabeth A. Mulroy (Dover, Mass.: Auburn House Publishing Co., 1988), pp. 99–122.

21. Jane Riblett Wilkie, "The Decline in Men's Labor Force Participation and Income and the Changing Structure of Family Economic Support," *Journal of Marriage and the Family* 53, No. 1 (February 1991): 111–122.

22. Ibid., p. 113.

23. Ibid., p. 115.

24. U.S. Bureau of the Census, "The Black Population in the United States: March 1990 and 1989," *Current Population Reports*, Series P-20, No. 448 (Washington, D.C.: U.S. Government Printing Office, 1990), p. 5.

25. Sylvia Ann Hewlett, *When the Bough Breaks: The Cost of Neglecting Our Children* (New York: Basic Books, 1991).

26. U.S. Bureau of the Census, "The Black Population in the United States," p. 14.

27. Wilkie, "The Decline in Men's Labor Force Participation and Income," p. 117.

28. Hewlett, *When the Bough Breaks*, p. 49.

29. U.S. Bureau of the Census, "The Black Population in the United States," p. 12.

30. Hewlett, *When the Bough Breaks*, p. 49.

31. Mark Fischetti, "Future Shock Meets the Photonics Workplace," *Photonics* (August 1993): 66–74.

—3—

Families and the Affordable Housing Crisis

> Shelter, the most significant mediator between each household and the larger society, putting each in touch with each other, is never a simple matter in a complex society, determining as it does access to many other necessities: education, work, social life, and political participation.
>
> Constance Perin[1]

A reduction in the availability of low-cost housing and the physical and social deterioration of living conditions in America's cities have made housing and neighborhood environments critical issues for one-parent families in the 1990s. Housing has unique economic, psychological, and symbolic significance that has a profound and pervasive impact on the quality of life beyond just the provision of shelter.

This chapter first examines the relationship between family stability and housing. Then four questions are posed that examine critical aspects of the housing crisis: (1) What has happened to America's cities? (2) Why are housing prices so high, and what are the impacts on low-wage families? (3) What is the role of race, class, and gender in patterns of housing segregation? and (4) How do we explain homelessness?

FAMILY AND COMMUNITY: WHY IS HOUSING IMPORTANT?

Long before the impacts of the housing crisis of the 1980s were visible, some researchers pointed with concern and interest to the effects of living conditions on the mental health of children. Stability in family living conditions was found to be a strong determinant of child development.[2] Divorce, death, or abandonment by a parent; changes in household composition; frequent residential mobility; irregular workforce patterns of a parent; and remarriage of parents have indirect effects on children.[3] The linkages between urban poverty and housing problems, and urban poverty and mental health problems are well documented.[4]

Experts debate which aspects of the urban environment are most harmful to the mental health of children. Some argue that it may be "overload"—the combined effects of multiple environmental stressors such as housing deprivation, victimization and fear of neighborhood crime, crowding, noise, density, and social isolation.[5] Others suggest that the critical factor for children may be the double burden of experiencing *both* the accumulation of stressful events in their own lives and living in communities characterized by high rates of stress.[6]

A growing body of evidence points to the importance of both life stressors and social resources in family functioning, and the value of measuring housing and neighborhood environment in this regard.[7] Psychiatrists have been chastised for not paying enough attention to aspects of housing and neighborhood environment that might influence mental health. Urban planners, architects, engineers, politicians, and public administrators—who hold responsibility for creating the "built" environment—have been equally chastised for showing only minimal interest in the human consequences of their activities in terms of mental health.[8]

Housing cost, quality, location, safety, unit density, and maintenance are features of community life that can impair or enhance family functioning.[9] Those living in deteriorating urban neighborhoods are tangled in a web of circumstance: landlords who raise rents and evict; banks that "redline" (the systematic disinvestment by mortgage lending institutions in targeted urban areas); suburban communities that prohibit construction of low-income housing; elected officials who slash affordable housing program budgets; absentee landlords who abandon properties rather than repair them. Forced residential mobility, so-called displacement, is common. Homelessness is the final form of housing displacement. Psychiatrist Matthew Dumont testified in a lawsuit brought by the Massachusetts Coalition for the Homeless versus Michael Dukakis, then governor, on the psychological significance of housing for single parents and children who are homeless:

The fear of losing one's home, of being "on the streets" . . . is not merely the threat of exposure to the elements. The biological need for protection from intemperate weather can be satisfied by public shelters, waiting rooms, and even doorways. What gives the experience its particular horror, particularly among mothers of young children, is a whole ecology of stressed realities. At some deep and central level of our emotional lives, we all carry a sense of dread that we will someday be alone and abandoned in the world. . . . The existence of a "home," an address, a place where someone we know can always be found, where we belong, is the only source of solace for that universal dread. Every homeless mother and child carries within them an empty space where the solace can be found in the rest of us. . . . Homeless children are subjected to the interruption of their schooling, the loss of their friends, malnutrition, and infection. The loss of a child's home is nothing less than an invitation to chronic illness. [10]

Family deterioration then, within the context of living in physically and socially deteriorating neighborhoods and of being homeless, should hardly be surprising.

HOUSING ATTRIBUTES

Because housing is more than shelter, and the quality and physical condition of housing promotes health and human development, some argue that housing is a basic need and should be a constitutional right.[11] Housing provides residents with space and an environment to meet a variety of needs such as eating, sleeping, cooking, and washing. It provides facilities for working, caring for children, and entertaining. Housing also satisfies psychological needs for privacy and quiet.[12]

Housing can be distinguished from other necessities such as food, clothing, and medical care in two ways. First, housing is a bulky, immobile, and durable good that can rarely be purchased in amounts other than whole dwelling units and usually is used over a considerable period of time. These characteristics make it difficult for families to alter patterns of consumption as they can with food, clothing, or medical care. Sudden changes in the income of a family, especially downward changes, are generally reflected in the purchase of less food, fewer clothes, or fewer or no medical services. Housing, on the other hand, is a fixed cost. The monthly rent or mortgage payment must be paid in full. It cannot be postponed or families will be evicted. If property taxes or rents go up, the family cannot give up the living room to reduce housing costs.

Second, cost affects the overall standard of living and determines where a family can live. This relationship influences (1) the physical condition and quality of the home, (2) the amount of space they will have, and (3) locational choice: the type of community and neighborhood they will live in. The amount a household can pay for housing directly affects its access to commercial facilities, quality schools, employment opportunities, public facilities, public and social services, recreational and cultural opportunities, the character of the immediate physical and social environment, and the availability of transportation networks to other points in a metropolitan area. No other purchasing decision has such far-reaching consequences.[13]

Most urban housing is geographically situated on streets where neighborhood conditions also determine the quality of living environments. The deteriorating condition of many urban residential neighborhoods is of great concern to single mothers because one-parent families are concentrated there, primarily in central cities.[14]

WHAT HAPPENED TO AMERICA'S CITIES?

Since the 1970s, urban areas in the United States and in other industrialized nations have been subjected to a series of unprecedented changes, the two most fundamental being restructuring of the economic base and massive shifts in populations across metropolitan regions.[15] These changes altered how cities were run, how federal aid to cities was calculated and politically dispersed, and what values and public priorities were shifted in city, state, and federal budget allocations. Indeed, such urban change resulted from the convergence of many economic, social, and political factors. Two elements of this urban transition relative to single-parent families are analyzed here: (1) the emergence of distressed neighborhoods where residents have become socially isolated, and (2) the changing demographics of urban populations, primarily the increase of minorities and the racial and ethnic mix it has created.

Distressed Neighborhoods and Isolated Deprivation

Concentrated poverty has increased in some urban neighborhoods, creating very distressed central areas. These are extremely poor neighborhoods in which 40 percent or more of the population is living below the poverty line.[16] There are already 36 million Americans living in poverty, including more than one in five children. Infant mortality has reached Third World levels in some urban neighborhoods. There are diverse causes, but some shifts are related, despite their different origins. The following five trends are discussed next: development of the suburbs, corporate flight, redlining, federal cutbacks in urban aid, and crime and illegal drugs.

The Suburbs. Post–World War II transportation policies subsidized highway construction from central cities to the suburbs, dividing numerous city working-class neighborhoods in the process. Housing policies offered government-insured mortgages to white suburbia (but not to cities), while urban renewal policies bulldozed city neighborhoods for construction of high-rise luxury housing and office building development displacing blue-collar families as a result. "White flight" out of declining urban neighborhoods to the suburbs was facilitated and even encouraged by public policies that subsidized such relocation.

Corporate Flight. The impacts of the global economy and of economic restructuring have directly produced a declining ability of blue- and many white-collar workers to provide economic support for their families. This is caused by *spatial reorganization,* that is, the relocation of manufacturing to suburban, exurban, and rural areas resulting in the ghettoization of central cities. In effect, jobs are more mobile than the urban poor.[17]

The effects of this spatial redevelopment caused by corporate flight are reflected in changes in the urban occupational structure. There has been a rise in economic activity that is not full-time, but part-time, casual labor. For example, since 1980, the Fortune 500 industrial companies have dropped 3.9 million employees from their payrolls. South-central Los Angeles and nearby areas lost 70,000 high-paying manufacturing jobs between 1978 and 1982 alone. Firms such as General Motors and Bethlehem Steel relocated or closed their plants. The only growth in the Los Angeles manufacturing sector is in the number of textile sweatshops that employ mostly undocumented immigrants at less than minimum wage.[18]

The increase in nonstandard forms of work means more women are in the labor market, but the low-waged work dictates that at least two household members must be wage earners to avoid poverty.[19]

Redlining. Many insurance companies and banks habitually deny loans to home buyers and small business entrepreneurs in certain urban areas. Although redlining was made illegal by the Community Reinvestment Act of 1977, it still persists, resulting in a self-fulfilling prophecy of urban decline.

Federal Cutbacks. The policy of New Federalism under the Reagan-Bush administration changed the terrain of intergovernmental relations and reversed a half-century of federal aid to cities. As the consequences of urban restructuring were taking effect, the Reagan-Bush administration did not develop federal legislation to ameliorate the social and economic dislocation associated with substantial shifts in capital and population.[20] Under the public pronouncement of "get the government off the backs of the people,"

Figure 3.1
Federal Spending Trends in the Reagan Era

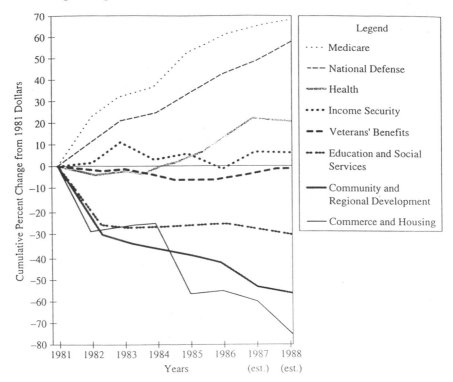

Source: Jennifer Wolch and Michael Dear, *Malign Neglect: Homelessness in an American City* (San Franciso, CA.: Jossey-Bass Publishers, 1993), p. 11.

the administration presided over the largest defense buildup in U.S. history, shifting resources away from social spending (see Figure 3.1). Strategies of federalism and privatization were used. First, the administration sought to divest the federal government of its responsibility for social programs and referred the task to state governments. Second, program implementation was privatized to nongovernmental providers whenever possible. By 1990, this approach successfully worked to diminish the federal role in urban policy. The shock effects were immediate. Between 1982 and 1985, federal programs targeted to the poor were cut by $57 billion, adjusted for inflation.[21]

By cutting federal aid to cities and eliminating federal revenue sharing, the share of federal dollars in city budgets was reduced to 5 percent in 1992, down from 14.3 percent in 1980. Successful programs such as urban economic development, job training, housing, health and nutrition, and education were cut by 70 percent. The already marginal standard of living of the poor was further eroded by loss of benefits through restricted eligibility requirements in public welfare programs. Some states made up part of the gap in the mid-1980s, but by the early 1990s state and city budgets were themselves bare bones. Essential services including fire, police, schools, and public works were drastically cut.[22]

Cuts in federal aid to cities had serious regional implications. Especially hard hit were cities in the northeastern, industrial "rustbowl." First, such cities were already coping with significant change: (1) white flight to the suburbs and to the Sunbelt; (2) corporate flight to the Sunbelt and offshore; and (3) large waves of immigration of minorities with limited education. Second, new urban jobs were in the information and service sectors, where unskilled, poorly educated minorities—the left-behind populations from white flight and corporate flight—were mismatched for these new urban growth industries. The regional disparity for black males is startling. David Stoesz (1988) points out that if the unemployment rate is combined with the labor force nonparticipation rate, in 1985 68 percent of young black males living in the Northeast were unemployed or not in school or not working, compared to 38.9 percent who lived in the West.[23]

Federal policies to deregulate the financial industry and the subsequent bailout of the savings and loan industry also have regional implications for cities. Stoesz points out that $300 to $500 billion will be paid to bail out savings and loan depositors over the next ten years in an unprecedented intranational transfer of funds. Because S & L conservatorships tend to be located in the Sunbelt, thirty-seven states will finance the liquidation of debt incurred in the remaining thirteen. Of these, Texas will receive 43.2 percent of the gross bailout funds, followed by Arkansas (7 percent), Florida (6.8 percent), California (6.7 percent), New Mexico (5.1 percent), Louisiana (4.6 percent), and Arizona (4.2 percent).[24] The bulk of the transfer will be borne by the Northeast and Midwest—"rustbowl" regions trying to renew their economies—and dispersed to recipients in regions that experienced rapid job growth and newest physical capital during the 1980s.[25]

Crime and Illegal Drugs. There is an overall violent context to American life. Lessons of violence are glorified in television shows, videos, and the movies. Easy access to handguns, especially among young males, and a propensity to solve disputes through violent means have increased homicide rates in the United States.[26] By the summer of 1993, neighborhood violence in central cities resulted in accidental and intentional shootings of children—the ultimate form of child abuse and a sign of social disintegration from Los Angeles to New York, from Chicago to Miami. In some urban census tracts there are more black youths in jail than in college.[27] Moreover, the public sector is now paying an astronomical sum to incarcerate a young man after crimes have been committed as opposed to educating a child before adolescence. In Massachusetts, for example, it costs a statewide average of $24,442 a year to keep one inmate in jail, while the average public expenditure to educate one child is $5,034.[28]

Urban Populations

Minorities now account for more than half the population in many of the nation's largest cities. In some cities, the influx of recent immigrants is increasing minority populations in central cities. Between 1980 and 1990, the minority share of central city populations climbed from 35 to 40 percent.[29]

These minority populations must face the growing social and economic distress of their urban neighborhoods. Inner-city job opportunities are receding, particularly for young people; restructuring of the American economy has eliminated many traditional entry-level jobs in manufacturing and other industries located in cities; and suburbanization has moved entry-level service jobs farther from where minorities live.

Despite the increasing concentration of minorities in central cities, a growing number has been moving to the suburbs, particularly in large metropolitan areas. The trend is most pronounced in western cities and least pronounced in the North.[30] As the more affluent minorities move to the suburbs, a greater number of racial and ethnic minorities are left behind in central city neighborhoods of concentrated poverty and isolated deprivation.

THE HOUSING AFFORDABILITY SLIDE TO HOMELESSNESS

Despite the disparities between urban and suburban areas, a snapshot of housing in the United States would conclude that Americans are the best housed people in the world. Impressive strides in housing quality have been made since the teeming tenements of industrializing urban America many decades ago. Nevertheless, while homelessness is the most visible manifestation of America's housing crisis today, much of the problem remains hidden and cannot be documented.

The federal Department of Housing and Urban Development (HUD) measures housing quality in terms of (1) the physical adequacy of each dwelling (the plumbing, heating, electrical systems, and the kitchen and bathroom facilities), (2) the presence of overcrowding (more than one person per room), and (3) excessive costs (considered to be 30 percent of income for rent and 40 percent of income for mortgage and maintenance). By these standards, about 33 percent of all dwellings in the United States have a housing quality problem. Women who head households (including both the elderly and women with children under age 18) occupy over 40 percent of these problem-ridden dwellings.[31]

The underlying problem is affordability, the squeeze between incomes on the one hand and housing costs on the other. Single-parent families experience this squeeze to an extraordinary degree because of their dispro-portionately low incomes.

Shelter Affordability

Homeownership is the American Dream; the desire for homeownership is so strong that families who can afford to buy their own home do so rather than rent. But this dream is fading fast for a large segment of the middle class. Following World War II, the rate of homeownership rose steadily for three decades with the help of postwar federal housing programs. Since 1980, however, it has steadily declined. According to a recent census study, nearly half of American families could not afford to buy a median-priced house in the region where they lived. Moreover, 91 percent of all current renter families cannot afford to buy a home.[32]

The cost of owning one's home has skyrocketed. Between 1970 and 1986, the median price of a single-family home for the entire Northeast increased from about $25,000 to about $125,000—a 400-percent increase. The Census Bureau reported that the increase was 249 percent nationally, compared with a 183-percent increase in median family income. In 1973, it took about 25 percent of a young family's median income to pay a mortgage on an average priced home; today it takes over half the income.

The cost of renting has also skyrocketed, making it difficult for a young family to save enough for a down payment. As a result of the peak in rents in the 1980s, middle-income families have stayed put and have been competing with poor families for a diminishing supply of available apartments.

Figure 3.2
Housing Tenure of One-Parent and Two-Parent Households with Children

TWO-PARENT HOUSEHOLDS
WITH CHILDREN UNDER 18

ONE-PARENT HOUSEHOLDS
WITH CHILDREN UNDER 18

Rented
35.3%

Owned Home
27.2%

Owned Home
72.8%

Rented
64.7%

Source: Adapted from U.S. Bureau of the Census, "Marital Status and Living Arrangements: March 1990," *Current Population Reports*, P-20, No. 450, Fig 6.

Single Parents as Renter Households

Single parents generally rent; therefore, the cost, availability, physical condition, and location of rental housing are fundamentally important concerns to them. In 1990, two-thirds of one-parent families were renters compared with only one-third of two-parent families (see Figure 3.2).

In 1989, more than half of all poor renters paid at least 50 percent of their incomes for housing. The typical young single mother is paying 70 percent of her modest income just for rental housing.[33] This pushes many households to double up in order to share housing costs and reduce the rent burden, but at the same time it can create another housing problem, overcrowding. Still others are paying high rents for substandard units in unsafe neighborhoods.

While public and subsidized housing programs have existed for several decades to ease the rent burden on poor households, their effectiveness has been limited. The majority of low-income renter households do not receive any kind of federal, state, or local rent subsidy or live in public housing.[34]

How much can families be expected to pay for housing? Is the 30 percent standard a fair standard for all families? Some suggest that defining "affordable" as not more than 30 percent of a household's income has serious shortcomings.[35] Families with high incomes can generally pay more than 30 percent of income for housing and still have money left to adequately cover other basic needs. For example, a family with a household income of

$100,000 that pays 50 percent of its income for housing would still have $50,000 left to cover food, clothing, medical, transportation, and so on. A family earning $10,000 a year and paying 30 percent for rent would have only $7,000 left, probably far too little to cover all other basic needs.

The 30 percent standard does not account for the effects of family size. A family of seven can expect to have larger food, clothing, and medical expenses than a family of two. If both families earn $15,000 a year and each pays no more than 30 percent of income for rent, the larger family will be severely squeezed in meeting the basic needs of its individual family members. The seven-person family requires a much larger apartment than the two-person family, which costs more.

Another approach creates a sliding scale by taking the difference between a family's disposable income (i.e., their after-tax income) and the cost of nonshelter needs: higher income families can afford to pay a higher percentage of their income than can lower income families; smaller households can afford to pay a higher percentage than larger households with the same income. People paying more than they can afford on this basis are "shelter poor"—the squeeze between inadequate incomes and excessive housing costs leaves them with insufficient money to meet their nonshelter needs at a minimum level.

The scale is somewhat different for single parents who receive public assistance, because their incomes are not taxable and they are eligible for noncash benefits such as Medicaid. Michael Stone (1993) found that in the Massachusetts housing market a single mother with two children who receives $510 a month of public assistance cannot afford to pay anything for housing and still meet her other needs at an adequate level. Even with food stamps and Medicaid, such families cannot afford to pay anything for shelter.[36]

The Housing Market

The growing income inequality between the rich and poor in the 1980s was starkly contrasted in how private real estate interests and federal and city governments responded to their respective housing needs. First, young, educated professionals found work in the growing service sector of America's cities. Often referring to themselves as "urban pioneers,"[37] they began viewing housing less as a home than as an investment, equally as valuable for its tax benefits as for its architectural details. They moved back into city neighborhoods close to the urban core to purchase and renovate rundown and devalued properties. Then they sold them for sizable profit.

Second, as the poor and the upper-income urban professionals began to compete for scarce inner-city housing, prices skyrocketed. Low-rent apartments were converted to luxury condominiums. Rooming houses (often referred to as single room occupancy hotels, or SROs)—the last bastion of residence for single poor people—were torn down or converted into expensive apartments. Businesses that used to cater to working poor families were replaced by upscale shops catering to the affluent.[38]

Third, the private housing market did not expand the number of affordable rental apartments during the 1980s primarily because it was not profitable to build rental property for the poor. Federal housing programs existed that could subsidize developers to build rental housing so that it was affordable to the poor and profitable for the developer. But during the Reagan and Bush administrations, the federal budget for affordable housing was cut by 70 percent. The outcome was a dwindling of new federally subsidized apartments from over 200,000 in the 1970s to fewer than 20,000 in 1990.[39] Thus, the supply of affordable rental housing was reduced just as the demand for it was increasing.

Fourth, the housing subsidy that was not eliminated in the 1980s is the one that benefits the rich—the federal tax code that allows homeowners to deduct all property tax and mortgage interest from their income taxes. Wealthy families are most likely to own their own homes and to itemize deductions; many have two homes. As a result, over 80 percent of households with annual incomes over $200,000 receive a homeowner tax deduction, while fewer than 1 percent of households with incomes below $10,000 get this subsidy. In 1991 alone, this subsidy cost the federal government $47 billion, more than four times the Department of Housing and Urban Development's budget for low-income housing.[40]

Residential Discrimination

Not all rental housing problems can be reduced to housing affordability or housing supply. Housing discrimination has long been a problem for people of color; cohabitating, unmarried partners; families with children; and low-income female-headed families. Some argue that the most injurious form of discrimination in housing is institutional racism, practiced for decades in government programs and through decisions and practices of real estate agents, landlords, financial institutions, and planning entities that regulate land use through zoning.[41] The manifestations of residential discrimination are observed in segregated central cities that are increasingly separate from nearby suburbs.

Central Cities and Segregation. The concentration of minorities in central cities is related to several factors. First, cities have historically been the port of entry for minority immigrants. Second, large industrial cities—where segregated neighborhoods were the rule—absorbed most of the millions of southern blacks who moved north after 1910. Third, discriminatory real estate practices and de facto segregation restrained the movement of minorities to the suburbs at the same time that whites were moving out of central city neighborhoods. Fourth, because minorities are disproportionately poor, they cannot afford to move to the suburbs.[42] In 1987, for example, minorities comprised 49 percent of residents in public or subsidized housing. About one in ten white renters lived in public or subsidized housing in 1987, compared with 29 percent of black, 27 percent of Native American, 16 percent of Latino, and 12 percent of Asian renters.[43]

Conventional government-sponsored, high-rise public housing projects built in the 1950s were often located in isolated urban areas as a result of fierce political battles in which working-class neighborhoods sought to keep the poor separate.[44] Once built, it soon became apparent that there were serious problems with this public housing approach. The sheer density and scale of these buildings concentrated the poor into housing ghettos and removed the supportive networks and social interactions available in existing neighborhoods. Moreover, these public housing residents were physically removed from the growing suburban job opportunities of the 1960s and 1970s.[45] Efforts to bring low-income families to the jobs by opening up the suburbs to public housing (even with low-density, scattered-site approaches) were, and continue to be, met with intense resistance.[46]

Suburban Land-Use Control. Increasing portions of suburban territory are no longer in the public realm, but are conceived, built, and marketed as private refuges without responsibility for a larger society.[47] For example, land-use controls are developed through zoning ordinances and building codes that exclude and protect suburban resources from newcomer populations. Those newcomers perceived to be the least desirable are low-income families, who some public administrators argue may cost the jurisdiction more in facilities and services.[48]

To many, the suburbs have come to mean the final stage in a natural, housing/life cycle order.[49] A family moves through stages of the life cycle in an ordered progression, like a ladder-of-life: (1) Newlyweds live in a rented apartment; (2) they work and save to purchase a condominium; (3) when the children are born, they move up to the top of the ladder and purchase a single-family house; (4) once the children are out of the house, the empty nesters may *choose* to move down the ladder by relocating to a retirement or lifecare community.[50]

Affordable housing in the suburbs challenges the ladder-of-life order because low-income households, especially one-parent families, are perceived to be jumping over prescribed categories without spending the requisite housing or life-cycle time. They move from poor urban renter to suburban renter, or even more brashly from homelessness to suburban renter.

The societal value guiding local housing and community development policies is the perception that households of different economic status would not choose to be neighbors. There is too little in common in terms of life interests, social behaviors, and aspirations. In practice, local zoning ordinances based on this perception permit exclusionary uses of prime residential property. Reflecting community norms, the concept of "mixing" is unnatural and undesirable.

The resulting landscape is soon overcome with problems: low-density development; inadequate services; and social, economic, racial, and ethnic segregation.[51] Thus, public decisions that control physical space in a community are used to reinforce social distance and limit contact between residents perceived to be different.

Racial and Economic Integration in the Suburbs. Racial and economic residential integration is rarely attempted in a systematic, institutionalized way. One notable exception is a project called the Gautreaux Program, a highly unusual experiment in racial and economic intergration in the Chicago metropolitan area. In the *Gautreaux* case, decided by the Supreme Court in 1976, the Court addressed racial discrimination in public housing. The Gautreaux Program is the major initiative adopted by the courts to provide a metropolitan-wide remedy for discrimination in Chicago's public housing. The program is one of the most extensive housing desegregation efforts in the history of this country.

Through the Gautreaux Program, a coordinating group called the Leadership Council for Metropolitan Area Communities locates apartments and arranges for participants to receive Section 8 rent subsidies. The program helps low-income black families who lived in public housing or were on public housing waiting lists to move into better housing in many kinds of neighborhoods, including largely black city areas, integrated city areas, and predominantly white middle-class suburbs throughout the six-county Chicago metropolitan area. Since the late 1970s, the program has placed over 3,800 families in private-sector apartments—more than half in the suburbs.[52]

Results of research on children and mothers who participated in the Gautreaux Program show satisfaction with their new communities and positive outcomes for both children and mothers. First, suburban movers cite profound benefits in their children's lives through better schools and a safer environment. Second, because the Gautreaux Program is a housing and not an employment program, it is significant that suburban movers were about 13 percent more likely than city movers to have a job post-move. These findings suggest that, to some extent, personal handicaps of low educational attainment and lack of job skills, as well as institutional work disincentives inherent in the public welfare system, can be overcome by improved opportunities.

For example, many participants found that there were more jobs available in the suburbs. Others said that the safer environment made it easier to work because they could leave school-aged children alone. Improved neighborhood safety, better role models, and a less depressing environment all appear to make it easier for these participants to find jobs. Overall, results indicate that low-income blacks get along quite well in white suburbs. They benefit from suburban schools, and they make friends and are accepted by many suburban neighbors. Neighborhoods make a great difference in their quality of life.[53]

A measure of the Gautreaux Program's success lies in its structural support of the housing search process. The national Section 8 program is based on a laissez-faire approach to housing search; that is, all searchers are on their own to locate a suitable apartment and bargain for their own tenant selection. While residential integration is one of the policy goals of Section 8, existing studies do not find a pattern of movement from segregated to integrated census tracts by people with Section 8 certificates.[54] Racial and class barriers encountered by other low-income black mothers in a housing search are buffered for Gautreaux participants by council staff who locate apartments (and thus willing landlords) on their behalf.

Explaining Homelessness

Changes in the economy, reduction in welfare programs, and the reduced supply of affordable housing described above were all contributing factors to homelessness for economically marginal people. The process of homelessness involves the interaction of three elements, according to Wolch, Dear, and Akita (1988). The first is a set of structural factors operating at state and national levels over the long term that include changes in the economy and reductions in public welfare benefits which, in effect, increase

Figure 3.3
Path to Homelessness: Structural and Personal Factors

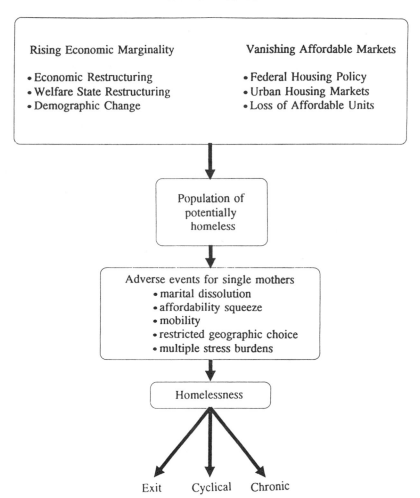

Rising Economic Marginality

• Economic Restructuring
• Welfare State Restructuring
• Demographic Change

Vanishing Affordable Markets

• Federal Housing Policy
• Urban Housing Markets
• Loss of Affordable Units

Population of
potentially
homeless

Adverse events for single mothers
 • marital dissolution
 • affordability squeeze
 • mobility
 • restricted geographic choice
 • multiple stress burdens

Homelessness

Exit   Cyclical   Chronic

Source: Adapted from Figure 1.1 in J. Wolch and M. Dear, *Malign Neglect: Homelessness in an American City* (San Francisco, Calif.: Jossey-Bass Publishers, 1993), p. 2.

the demand for temporary shelter (see Figure 3.3). The second set of structural factors are those described above that reduced the supply of affordable housing such as urban renewal, gentrification, and exclusionary zoning. The third set focuses on the individual to account for particular adverse events that propel people into homelessness. The five most common immediate causes that individuals report are eviction, discharge from an institution, loss of a job, personal crisis (including divorce and domestic violence), and removal of a monetary or nonmonetary welfare support.[55]

Low-wage, economically marginal single-mother families are susceptible to a housing affordability slide that illustrates these structural and personal factors. The slide has four elements. First, it begins with a housing affordability squeeze created by the gap between a mother's low level of income and the high cost of rental housing. Her economic marginality may be caused by separation and divorce, low wages, and/or nonreceipt of child support. This economic problem precipitates the second element, frequent residential mobility, in an attempt to locate less expensive accommodation. The consequence of frequent residential mobility, however, is family destabilization and insecurity. Third, residential discrimination reduces low-income single mothers' choices of where they can live. A consequence of reduced choice in freedom to move, particularly for black and Hispanic women, is the concentration of such families in urban neighborhoods with lower cost rental housing but also with higher crime rates, unsafe streets, and more neighborhood violence. Fourth, this downward spiral, a vicious cycle of deteriorating circumstance and living conditions, ends in multiple stress burdens for families now demoralized by life on the streets, evictions, court appearances, and homeless shelters. As psychiatrist Matthew Dumont has remarked, "Of all life's grating events, of all the stressors which drive people crazy, the loss of one's home ranks at the top."[56]

In effect, homelessness is the bottom rung of the rental housing crisis for the economically marginal who have the fewest economic and social supports.[57]

SUMMARY

This chapter has analyzed recent trends in housing and urban development in order to explain how the physical environment has been restructured over the past twenty years. The chapter began by pointing out that housing has unique properties beyond shelter that make it central to the well-being of all families with children: safety, security, and stability. Housing affordability, the increased cost of renting and homeownership for those with lowered incomes, is a key reason why housing has become an important factor for one-parent families in the 1990s. Because single-parent families are predominantly renter households, the crisis in affordable rental housing has adversely affected them.

The convergence of the race, class, and gender of single parents results in patterns of residential segregation for economically marginal single mothers. Racial discrimination affects low-income black and Hispanic residents of central cities who seek to improve their housing and neighborhood environments by relocating to the suburbs or other locations that have the amenities and opportunities they seek. Today some urban neighborhoods in American cities are islands of concentrated deprivation and isolation for left-behind, often single-mother families.

Long-term structural factors account for a decline in the physical and social condition of America's cities; an increase in demand for affordable housing; and a decline in supply of such housing—all contributing to homelessness. In combination with immediate, adverse personal events such as domestic violence, separation and divorce, eviction, or job layoffs, a downward spiral is precipitated and the path to homelessness is difficult to reverse.

NOTES

1. Constance Perin, *Everything in Its Place: Social Order and Land Use in America* (Princeton, N.J.: Princeton University Press, 1977).

2. See, for example, Uri Bronfenbrenner, "Ecology of the Family as Context for Human Development: Research Perspectives," *Developmental Psychology* 22 (1986): 723–742; and L. Richards, "The Precarious Survival and Hard-Won Satisfactions of White Single Parent Families," *Family Relations* 38 (1989): 396–403.

3. Bronfenbrenner, "Ecology of the Family," pp. 723–742.

4. See, for example, Jon Pynoos, Robert Schafer, and Chester W. Hartman, eds., *Housing Urban America* (New York: Aldine Publishing Co., 1980); J. Comer and H. Hill, "Social Policy and the Mental Health of Black Children," *Journal of the American Academy of Child Psychiatry* 24 (1985): 175–181; and H. Freeman, "Psychiatric Aspects of Environmental Stress," *International Journal of Mental Health* 17 (1988): 13–23; and D. Belle, "Poverty and Women's Mental Health," *American Psychologist* 45 (1990): 385–389.

5. Freeman, "Psychiatric Aspects of Environmental Stress," pp. 13– 23.

6. A. Linsky and M. Straus, *Social Stress in the United States: Links to Regional Patterns in Crime and Illness* (Dover, Mass.: Auburn House Publishing Co., 1986).

7. See, for example, M. Rutter, "Psychosocial Resilience and Protective Mechanisms," *American Journal of Orthopsychiatry* 57 (1987): 316–331; and R. Moos and B. Moos, *Life Stressors and Social Resources Inventory Preliminary Manual* (Palo Alto, Calif.: Social Ecology Laboratory, Stanford University and Veterans' Administrative Medical Center, 1990).

8. Freeman, "Psychiatric Aspects of Environmental Stress," pp. 13– 23.

9. See, for example, O. Newman, *Community of Interest* (Garden City, N.Y.: Anchor Press/Doubleday, 1980); W. Rohe, "Urban Planning and Mental Health," *Prevention in Human Services* 4 (1985): 79–110; Jacqueline Leavitt, "The Shelter-Service Crisis and Single Parents," *The Unsheltered Woman: Women and Housing in the 1980's*, ed. Eugenie Birch (New Brunswick, N.J.: Center for Urban Policy Research, 1985); and A. Kotlowitz, *There Are No Children Here: A Story of Two Boys Growing Up in the Other America* (New York: Doubleday Publishing Co., 1991).

10. Affidavit of Matthew P. Dumont, M.D., in *Massachusetts Coalition for the Homeless vs. Dukakis*, Suffolk Superior Court, Civil No. 80109, May 5, 1986, pp. 4–6.

11. Frank I. Smizik and Michael E. Stone, "Single-Parent Families and a Right to Housing," in *Women as Single Parents: Confronting Institutional Barriers in the Courts, the Workplace, and the Housing Market*, ed. Elizabeth A. Mulroy (Dover, Mass.: Auburn House Publishing Co., 1988), pp. 227–270.

12. Leavitt, "The Shelter-Service Crisis," pp. 153–176.

13. Smizik and Stone, "Single-Parent Families," pp. 227–270.

14. Steve Rawlings, "Single Parents and Their Children," U.S Bureau of the Census, "Studies in Marriage and the Family," *Current Population Reports*, Series P-23, No. 162 (Washington, D.C.: U.S. Government Printing Office, 1989), Table H, p. 21.

15. M. Gottdiener and Chris G. Pickvance, eds., *Urban Life in Transition, Urban Affairs Annual Reviews* 39 (Newbury Park, Calif.: Sage Publications, 1991).

16. Mark A. Hughes, "Employment Decentralization and Accessibility: A Strategy for Stimulating Regional Mobility," *Journal of the American Planning Association* 57, No. 3 (Summer 1991): 288–298.

17. Bryan R. Roberts, "Household Coping Strategies and Urban Poverty in a Comparative Perspective," in *Urban Life in Transition, Urban Affairs Annual Reviews* 39, eds. M. Gottdiener and C. Pickvance (Newbury Park, Calif.: Sage Publications, 1991), p. 149.

18. Peter Dreier, "Bush to Cities: Drop Dead," *The Progressive* 56, No. 7 (July 1992): 22.

19. Roberts, "Household Coping Strategies," pp. 149–151.

20. D. Stoesz, "The Fall of the Industrial City: The Reagan Legacy for Urban Policy," *Journal of Sociology and Social Welfare* 19, No. 1 (1992): 149–167, Special Issue on the Reagan Legacy and the American Welfare State.

21. Jennifer Wolch and Michael Dear, *Malign Neglect* (San Francisco: Jossey-Bass Publishers, 1993), p. 11.

22. Ibid., pp. 20–23.

23. Stoesz, "The Fall of the Industrial City," p. 155.

24. Ibid., p. 158.

25. Hill, as quoted in Stoesz, "The Fall of the Industrial City."

26. Deborah Prowthrow-Stith, *Deadly Consequences* (New York: HarperCollins, 1991), p. 15.

27. Ibid., p. 134.

28. Massachusetts Department of Corrections and Massachusetts Department of Education, Office of Research, as reported to the Massachusetts Budget Bureau for fiscal year 1993.

29. William P. O'Hare, "America's Minorities—The Demographics of Diversity," *Population Bulletin* 47, No. 4 (December 1992): 25.

30. Ibid., p. 27.

31. Birch, *The Unsheltered Woman*, pp. 21–45.

32. Peter Dreier and Richard Applebaum, "The Housing Crisis Enters the 1990's," *New England Journal of Public Policy* 8, No. 1 (Spring/Summer 1992): 155–167. Special Issue on Homelessness: New England and Beyond, ed. Padraig O'Malley.

33. Ibid.

34. U.S. Bureau of the Census, "Housing Characteristics of Selected Races and Hispanic-Origin Households in the United States: 1987," Series H121–87–1 (Washington, D.C.: U.S. Government Printing Office, 1990), p. 31.

35. Cushing N. Dolbeare, *Out of Reach: Why Everyday People Can't Find Affordable Housing* (Washington, D.C.: Low Income Housing Information Service, September 1991).

36. Michael Stone, *Shelter Poverty: New Ideas on Affordable Housing* (Philadelphia: Temple University Press, 1993).

37. For an interesting discussion of urban neighborhood change from the perspective of higher income households who consider themselves "urban pioneers," see M. A. Morrill, "A Boston Townhouse," *Victorian Homes* (Winter 1993), pp. 35–40.

38. Dreier and Applebaum, "The Housing Crisis," pp. 155–167.

39. Ibid.

40. Ibid.

41. Robert D. Bullard and Joe R. Feagin, "Racism and the City," in *Urban Life in Transition, Urban Affairs Annual Reviews* 39, eds. M. Gottdiener and C. Pickvance (Newbury Park, Calif.: Sage Publications, 1991), pp. 61–68.

42. O'Hare, "America's Minorities," p. 27.

43. U.S. Bureau of the Census. "Housing Characteristics of Selected Races and Hispanic-Origin Households," Table 4.

44. M. Myerson and E. C. Banfield, *Politics, Planning and the Public Interest: The Case of Public Housing in Chicago* (Glencoe, Ill.: Free Press, 1955).

45. E. J. Meehan, *The Quality of Federal Policy Making: Programmed Failure in Public Housing* (Columbia: University of Missouri Press, 1979).

46. For example, see Nina Gruen and Claude Gruen, *Low and Moderate Income Housing in the Suburbs* (New York: Praeger, 1972); A. Downs, *Opening Up the Suburbs* (New Haven, Conn.: Yale University Press, 1973); and Alexander

Polikiff, *Housing the Poor: The Case for Heroism* (Cambridge, Mass.: Ballinger Press, 1978).

47. E. Blakely and D. Ames, "Changing Places: American Urban Policy for the 1990's," *Journal of Urban Affairs* 14, No. 314 (1992): 399–422.

48. Perin, *Everything in Its Place*, pp. 32–80.

49. Ibid.

50. Ibid.

51. Robert W. Lake, "Rethinking NIMBY," *American Planning Association Journal* 59, No. 1 (Winter 1993): 87–93.

52. James Rosenbaum and Susan Popkin, "Economic and Social Impacts of Housing Integration," *Research and Policy Reports*, Center for Urban Affairs and Policy Research (Evanston, Ill.: Northwestern University, March 1990).

53. James Rosenbaum and Susan Popkin, "The Gautreaux Program: An Experiment in Racial and Economic Integration, *The Center Report: Current Policy Issues* 2, No. 1 (Spring 1990): 4 (Evanston, Ill.: Northwestern University).

54. Rosenbaum and Popkin, "The Gautreaux Program," p. 1; and Elizabeth A. Mulroy, "The Search for Affordable Housing," in *Women As Single Parents: Confronting Institutional Barriers in the Courts, the Workplace, and the Housing Market*, ed. Elizabeth A. Mulroy (Dover, Mass.: Auburn House Publishing Co., 1988), pp. 123–164.

55. For a thorough analysis of the causes and consequences of homelessness, see, for example, Jennifer R. Wolch, Michael Dear, and Andrea Akita, "Explaining Homelessness," *Journal of the American Planning Association* 54, No. 4 (Autumn 1988): 443–453; Elizabeth A. Mulroy, "The Housing Affordability Slide in Action: How Single Mothers Slip into Homelessness," *New England Journal of Public Policy* 8, No. 1 (Spring/Summer 1992): 203–214, Special Issue on Homelessness: New England and Beyond; and Jennifer Wolch and Michael Dear, *Malign Neglect: Homelessness in an American City* (San Francisco: Jossey-Bass, 1993).

56. Affidavit of Matthew P. Dumont, M.D., in *Massachusetts Coalition for the Homeless vs. Dukakis*, Suffolk Superior Court, Civil No. 80109, May 5, 1986, pp. 4–6.

57. For a fuller discussion of single mothers and the housing affordability slide to homelessness, see, for example, Elizabeth A. Mulroy and Terry S. Lane, "Housing Affordability, Stress and Single Mothers: Pathway to Homelessness," *Journal of Sociology and Social Welfare* 19, No. 3 (September 1992): 51–64; and Mulroy, "The Housing Affordability Slide in Action."

Part II

Meeting Basic Needs

The four chapters in this part present factual accounts of how a diverse population of single mothers experience life on a day-to-day basis in their dual roles of sole family provider and sole resident parent. Findings from a qualitative study of single mothers are introduced here in order to present the single mothers' own perspective. Emphasis is placed on their perceptions of their personal situations and living conditions, their coping strategies, and the outcomes of their decisions. Class and race differences are explored in each chapter.

Chapter 4 examines the role of domestic violence in relationship breakdown. Single mothers describe how domestic violence was a key factor in determining their single-parent status. Their interactions with ex-spouses, partners, family members, friends, the police, and the court system are presented.

In Chapter 5, single mothers explain how employment outside the home comes at a high price, considering multiple barriers that must be overcome. The financial costs of child care, transportation, clothing, health benefits, and taxes are weighed against low-wage expectations. Additional barriers include the psychic costs of role-overload, diminished time for parenting, sexual harassment at the workplace, and the geographic dilemma posed by the mismatch between where the jobs are, where single mothers live, and where affordable child care is located.

Chapter 6 focuses on the housing context of teen mothers who live in urban poverty. It examines the effects of the role played by the families of origin, the fathers of the babies, housing policies and regulations, and the mothers' personal coping strategies not only on housing outcomes, but also on educational and social support opportunities.

In Chapter 7 the divorced and separated explain the pivotal role housing plays in their lives. Building on background material presented in Chapter 3, we trace the relationship between disposition of the marital home and the process of housing resettlement. Case examples help to illustrate that when housing choices are most limited, displacement, frequent mobility, and family instability can become housing outcomes.

—4—

Lost Dreams: Domestic Violence and Relationship Breakdown

I got married at 18. I was brought up to be dependent—a princess on a pedestal. I was taught that men take care of women. But that lesson didn't prepare me for the real world. I always dreamed of living in a safe place—the suburbs—with good schools for my children and enough space for the whole family. My husband built us a beautiful home from scratch. About a year and a half into the marriage I got pregnant. That's when my husband started to become physically and violently abusive. The first time he beat me I was in the shower. He was a hard worker and a good provider, but the abuse got worse over time. He choked me, threw me around, pulled my hair, punched me. I stayed with him for six years. I stayed because I believed I had to honor my marriage vows, and because I didn't think I was self-sufficient enough to leave. Then I went to a counselor who helped me realize that my life was in danger and that I needed to leave . . .

Mary Zagreb, age 34

Children are brought up reading fairy tales and romantic stories of love, marriage, and eternal happiness. A beautiful yet vulnerable young princess is rescued by a handsome Prince Charming, and he carries her off to his castle where they live happily ever after. In modern times, the bride and groom also hope to live happily ever after. The American Dream of a single-family home in a safe, suburban neighborhood, which both husband and wife work hard to pay for and maintain, reflects status, stability, responsibility, and security.

For millions of women, however, their own home is also the most dangerous place they can be. According to the American Medical Association, the prevalence of domestic violence makes "the American home more dangerous to women than city streets."[1] The number of one-parent families will continue to rise in the 1990s as married and never-married women seek protection from violent behavior. Pregnant women and women with children seek safety, rergardless of their marital status.

This chapter examines the role of domestic violence in the breakdown of marital relationships. It discusses the scope of the problem; how it affects those who experience it, both married and unmarried, and how society is responding to it.

SCOPE OF THE PROBLEM

Domestic violence can happen to anyone. It spans racial, socioeconomic, and demographic boundaries. The statistics are alarming:

- Every 15 seconds a woman is battered.
- An estimated 2 to 4 million women are physically abused each year.
- In 1991, 28 percent of all female murder victims were slain by their husbands or boyfriends.
- The FBI reports that domestic violence is the number one cause of injury to women, more than rape, muggings, and auto accidents combined.
- Violence in the home exists in various forms in all societies afflicting women regardless of their social position, creed, race, or culture.[2]

Background

Domestic violence is not a new phenomenon. Historically, not only did the abuse of a wife by her husband exist, but it was often government sanctioned. Throughout medieval times, a husband was able to discipline his wife by corporal punishment and could even murder her. As late as the nineteenth century in England, husbands were not punished for murdering their wives. The United States, following English law, allowed a husband in the nineteenth century to physically discipline his wife "without subjecting himself to vexatious prosecutions for assault and battery, resulting in the discredit and shame of all parties concerned."[3] Thus evolved the colloquial expression "rule of thumb" whereby a husband could beat his wife with a "stick no bigger than his thumb." Not until the twentieth century did American courts begin to uphold laws that criminalize wife-beating. A change in societal attitudes about domestic violence was very slow to follow.

In previous decades, guilt, lack of money, dependency, and fear forced women to stay in abusive relationships. Mary Zagreb's situation is not unusual; she stayed for the traditional reason: she believed her marriage vows were a sacred commitment. It took her several years and the help of a counselor finally to accept the dangerous reality of her situation, a common reaction among battered women.

Domestic violence as a societal problem is just beginning to be understood. It remains a "hidden" crime shielded from public view behind a veneer of respectability—an intact, two-parent family form, a well-maintained property with properly pulled curtains and mowed lawns. In earlier decades, domestic violence was perceived as a private affair to be worked out between the spouses. Other family members, neighbors, and community agencies maintained a hands-off position. Even local police were reluctant to intervene when called to help in a volatile domestic matter. Police expressed futility and frustration with such cases when their efforts to arrest an abusive husband and bring him to court were thwarted by battered wives who did not show up at the court hearing to press charges.

An underlying rationale for a hands-off approach was the widespread assumption that a man was master of his household, an unquestioned authority figure in his own home. The cultural practice of a wife taking her husband's name at marriage to become Mrs. John Doe further reinforced her subservient and ancillary role, not only within the private domain of the family but also in the public domain of society and community life. In effect, she gave over her life to her husband. His public identity became her identity. He was the person; she was the "other."[4]

Women respond to the experience of domestic violence in very different ways depending on the level of family or other support, religious convictions, and financial resources. Some women leave their marriages right away; others stay for years. Many unmarried women who become pregnant do not have marriage as an option because the men leave. When the man does stay, but becomes abusive, many women decide to remain single rather than risk a lifetime of domestic violence.

As society's definition of family has expanded, so has the law's definition of domestic violence. While some states cling to the traditional view of domestic violence as between spouses or former spouses, legislatures and courts are expanding the scope of the law to include children, relatives, unmarried persons living together, persons with a child in common, and those of the same sex who are in a committed relationship.[5]

Root Causes of Abuse

Reinforced with the assumption of male privilege and superiority, men who batter often believe they have a right to hit their wives, to show her who is boss. Women who have been battered feel they have no basic human rights, often not even the right not to be hit. They equate dominance with masculinity. Moreover, such women believe their own feelings of self-worth are based on their ability to attract and maintain a relationship with a man. The socially and culturally sanctioned criteria for successful womanhood are first, to be selected by a man for marriage, and second, to hold the family together by maintaining the marital relationship. If this is her measure of success and means to achieve societal acceptance, many women will endure battering rather than suffer shame, guilt, and society's opprobrium for having failed at her primary role responsibility.

Many factors may contribute to the occurrence of domestic violence, but studies indicate that substance abuse, learned behavior, and trial-and-error learning are prominent. Some studies have found that 50 percent of abusive men use or are addicted to some substance.[6] Alcohol and other mood-altering drugs often reduce an individual's ability to control violent impulses.

Social learning theory suggests that people learn aggressive behavior by observing how others behave, especially parents and friends who command attention. Several studies have linked abusive behavior in men to their childhood homes where one or more of the children were victims of physical or sexual abuse, or where the mother was battered by her husband or boyfriend.[7]

Even men who did not grow up in a home where domestic violence was present learn to abuse women when they experience a positive outcome to controlling and subjugating women. Through trial and error, a man may find himself using violent behavior to put a temporary end to an immediate discomfort he feels in the relationship.

Types of Abuse

Domestic violence is the use or threat of physical violence by the abuser to gain control and power over the victim. While battering can be inflicted on any household member regardless of age, gender, or relationship, according to the U.S. Department of Justice approximately 95 percent of the victims of battering are women. There are three types of spousal abuse: physical abuse, sexual abuse, and psychological/emotional abuse.

Physical Abuse. Physical abuse is the most visible form of domestic violence. Behaviors characteristic of physical battering include kicking, hitting, biting, choking, pushing, and assaults with weapons. Sometimes certain areas of the body are targeted such as the abdomen of a pregnant woman. A common theme appears to be emerging: battering may begin or increase in severity during pregnancy. To illustrate this pattern, the experiences of Mary Zagreb and Catherine Rice are presented.

Mary Zagreb, whose story introduced this chapter, first experienced physical abuse from her husband when she became pregnant. Mary was able to move back home with her parents who were supportive of the separation. However, she did not know how to cope with the stress imposed by her husband's persistent anger toward her even after the separation. She found herself developing debilitating eating disorders. First, she became anorexic, and then she fought a five-year battle with bulimia. She describes her battle with bulimia to be more painful than anything she has ever experienced, including the abuse and the divorce. She could find no direction or support in her life to get over her confusion about the food addiction by herself. Her recovery began only after she joined a church that had numerous other single mothers in the congregation with whom she formed a community.

Catherine Rice left her marriage a lot sooner. She was only 20 when her husband "snapped" and beat her when she was pregnant. Although he seemed happy about the pregnancy at first, he was very violent anyway. He had hit her before, but never in the way he did as the pregnancy progressed. She is surprised that the baby survived at all. From Catherine's perspective, her husband resented the pending birth because it meant he had to change his behavior—be responsible, get a job, take care of a family—things she feels he did not want to do. She feels he is the one who wanted to be taken care of. They were living in Arizona at the time, and she moved 3,000 miles away to stay with a friend. He followed, but three years later neither she nor the child have any contact with him. He is "among the missing," she remarked.

Sexual Abuse. Sexual violence, or "marital rape," includes physical attacks on the victim's breasts or genitals, sexual sadism, and forced sexual activity. As in rape occurring outside the family, marital rape is an act of violence and aggression in which sex is the method used to humiliate, hurt, degrade, and dominate the woman.

Joan O'Connor experienced marital rape and also discovered that her husband was sexually abusing their daughter. Despite the trauma of the abuse, the situation was hard to leave—not because she did not want to leave, but because she and the children had nowhere to go. Joan was from a middle-class background. She lived in a single-family house in an affluent suburban community. She could not believe this was actually happening in her marriage. Yet at age 35 and with three young children, Joan finally did seek needed emergency housing in a battered women's shelter in the next town. She credits that resource with turning her and the children's lives around, especially her daughter's. If she needed that emergency shelter today, she could not get it. The shelter is full.

Psychological/Emotional Abuse. While physical and sexual abuse are the more overt types of abuse that bring women before the courts, the consequences of psychological/emotional abuse can be more traumatic and long-lasting; it is the systematic destruction of a person's self-esteem. It can involve economic exploitation by withholding money and household resources; the prevention of a wife from working or seeking education or training that could further her independence; the use of intimidation by violent outbursts of anger or threats of killing, suicide, or harming a child; or the extreme controlling of persons a woman can see or where she can go.

Whether the batterer is a male or female, the intent is the same: to feel dominant and superior in the relationship, while making the partner feel subordinate, incompetent, worthless, and anxious.[8] The next case examples illustrate how two formerly married women experienced the process of being emotionally abused.

At age 17, Darlene Sawyer got pregnant after a three-month relationship with a 23-year-old man, got married immediately, and thought she was living a fairy tale; "I thought I had died and gone to heaven. It didn't matter that life wasn't perfect. Big deal. I had my baby, a house to live in and food to eat. It was better than anything I had known before. I thought I had married a prince and was going to live happily ever after, but I never saw it."

She stayed married for sixteen years. At the age of 33 and with four children, the emotional and psychological abuse reached a point she could no longer tolerate. She credits a religious support group for giving her an outside perspective. She gained enough insight to examine her marriage for the first time. "I was shocked because I had never really thought about it. I thought I was as happy as you get, and I thought everybody was in an abusive home."

On reflection, Darlene sees her ex-husband as a Dr. Jekyll and Mr. Hyde. On the one hand, she remembers the verbal abuse, the disrespect, the restrictions. He would not let her brothers come to visit, and she became the prisoner he wanted. She recalls her husband's threats to kill her, how he hated her body change during pregnancy, the jealous threats to kill one of the children when she brought her home from the hospital as a newborn, the drinking and drugs that they did together. The greatest humiliation, however, was an affair he was having with a woman she knew, that he acknowledged and refused ever to end.

On the other hand, her former husband was always generous with money during the marriage. As a divorced man, he is providing child support; that has never been a problem. He now speaks to her without disrespect. She sees him as doing the best that he can. She believes that he just never learned how to love. Now at 40, Darlene looks back on her married life as isolated and lonely, a life she remembers selectively.

If I remembered everything, I would be insane. I never thought about whether or not I was happy. I had my own happiness through drinking. My husband loved me to be a drunk because then I was happy. I used "speed" because it kept me energetic enough to keep the house immaculate and that's what he liked. It kept me thin enough and that's what he liked.

However, when Darlene stopped drinking and doing drugs after joining her support group, she did not like the fact that her husband was still gambling, drinking, and doing drugs. The change in her behavior upset him and increased the abuse. He accused God of destroying their marriage. But Darlene explains, "I think God saw that I was disappearing, you know, that I wasn't a real person. I was just this robot doing something for somebody else all the time."

Darlene has remained at home taking care of her children for the seven years since the divorce. She is extremely anxious about seeking potential employment.

Darlene is actively involved in a counseling and support group in order to gain self-confidence.

My memory's not very good. . . . You really have to get your memory so you can feel like you can meet somebody's needs. A boss is like an abusive husband in my mind, even before I meet him. This is the man who is going to find fault with me, he's going to abuse me, and then he's going to fire me, and that is going to ruin my record. So I'm not even going to try. . . . [In work] I have to perform for someone. Well, I failed. Well I was not the perfect wife because I had a bad marriage. Even if it was his fault, I failed. I have never been able to get out from under the blame. If I was more perfect, he would have loved me. If I were a better mother, he would have loved his kids. There is no way that I feel I am an O.K. person anymore. Everything I worked so hard to attain I walked into. I lived a thousand years going in one direction and it fell apart. So now what?

Darlene's friend, Deborah Palimieri, stayed in her marriage until her husband finally filed for divorce. Her story reflects how strong religious beliefs influenced Deborah to stay in an abusive marriage regardless of the personal costs to her and her children.

The threat of physical abuse was always there. The threat of murder was always there. Verbal attacks about her incompetence were expressed daily. The mother of two children, Deborah has been separated now for two years and is waiting for a court date for a divorce hearing. She lives in constant fear. The greatest fear is that she will lose custody of her 12-year-old son. "He always threatens to take the children away from me, to prove that I'm an unfit mother," she reports.

Deborah believes she could never have had the courage to file for divorce herself, but she was jubilant when her husband finally did it. She didn't want to file for two reasons. First, she really thought things would get better. Second, she felt there would be retribution from her church in which she was raised: "I was almost fearful that if I filed for divorce I would be out of God's will. It's very imbedded in my heart. Rules and regulations. Biblically, it would be O.K. for him to ask for a divorce, but it might be going against God if I asked."

The problem with waiting passively for her husband to take action, however, was the toll the sixteen-year emotional and psychological abuse took on her own development. Deborah is starting to put her life back together, and describes the fragile turning point she confronted.

The problem is there are now so many emotional scars inside you have to deal with, that it makes it harder going on with your life. . . . It's just that inner struggle. No one knows that. People wonder why you're not working, why you are depressed, this and that—everything—and it's from the wounds. It's hard just getting up in the morning, doing simple chores. It takes a long time for the wounds to heal. But they do heal. I want to be a nurse. I want to be an adult. But I'm a child inside, and I have to be patient with myself. You come to a point where you have to decide—it's either going to be you or your sanity. You've got to pick one. And it's got to be you.

Those victims of domestic violence who turn to alcohol, drugs, or suicide at this critical turning point unfortunately pick the other option. In one study, battering accounted for 25 percent of suicide attempts by women and 50 percent of all suicide attempts by black women.[9] Experiencing an abusive, marital relationship is clearly very stressful.

Spillover Effects: Urban Violence, Teen Pregnancy, and Abusive Behavior

Young, urban black and Hispanic women speak of living in an environment of abuse where stressful urban street violence erupts into domestic violence and where men frequently leave their partners with unsupported children. At its core is the tension between young women's expectations to have a violence-free relationship with the father of their child in an environment where neighborhood violence, illegal drugs, gangs, guns, and incarceration spill over into unacceptable violence toward women, children, and men. This aspect of domestic violence exists outside traditional definitions of domestic abuse, yet currently represents a serious problem for black family formation.

For example, many pregnant black and Hispanic adolescent girls are now postponing marriage or not marrying at all, in large measure because they would rather stay single than endure a domestic partnership fraught with abuse. Sociologist William Julius Wilson (1987) has depicted a reduced field of marriageable urban black males in what he called the Male Marriageable Pool Index, the MMPI.[10] The declining unemployment of young black males, he suggests, contributes to their inability to be family breadwinners. The escalating levels of violence in America's inner cities in the 1990s among young men of color—homicides, incarceration, substance abuse, gangs—are further reducing the field of future husbands for inner-city young mothers.

What is not changing are the expectations young women have for a future partner and father for their child. They seek young men who are employable; can make a commitment; will love, care for, and support a child financially and emotionally; are not abusive; and are not doing or selling drugs. Their dilemma, some young women claim, is that the young men in their lives are not meeting these expectations. The men they know, their future partners, are caught in a web of neighborhood violence. They exhibit abuse toward women that puts off many teenage girls. According to one pregnant 18 year old, "The streets are taking the men." In this stressful personal and neighborhood environment, the best chance for their own and their child's survival, some young women reason, is the coping strategy to let go of the relationship and move on alone.

Marcia Taylor, a 17-year-old black woman with a newborn, observes the patterns of abuse this way: "The boys get rough and hit us to show off to their friends. Among the boys, they brag they want to 'show her who's the man.' Our boyfriends turn to their friends to reinforce macho behavior."

In addition to hitting, teenage girls point out other behaviors they consider part of the spillover effect: not acknowledging paternity, not visiting the newborn, not supporting the child, and controlling the girl's behavior—where she goes, what she does, whom she sees.

Nineteen-year-old Rosalie Smith says that one of the hardest things to cope with is the ridicule and rejection she and other girls experience once they've had a baby and they are pushing it in a stroller in the neighborhood. She considers this emotional abuse: "The guys are hanging out on the street and you go by. They laugh and joke about whose baby it is. 'Not mine, not mine' they say, like you've been sleeping with every one of them. It's humiliating. Boyfriends make promises, but they don't keep them. They leave. They're empty promises."

Rosalie believes that teenage girls and boys are both irresponsible if they conceive a child. But making the decision to have the baby rather than abort and then going through a pregnancy, Rosalie observes, a girl becomes mature and responsible, while boys do not seem to change. Rosalie, for instance, felt she was involved in a great relationship and that marriage was planned some day. Her boyfriend was happy when she got pregnant. By the second trimester of the pregnancy, however, he was on a downward spiral. He held a stable job before the pregnancy, but then his behavior began to change. She saw him move closer and closer to his friends hanging out on the street. Eventually, he was picked up and put in jail for doing and selling drugs. She says:

I realized this was a *big* risk. I could go ahead and marry him as he is, and deal with it, or leave it alone. But they don't change. I finally said to myself this isn't working. If he's going to be a part of the baby's life he'll be it on his own. I'm not going to keep saying to myself "She needs a father. . . . She needs a father." So I just finally let the whole thing go. He was my first real boyfriend. . . . I haven't had a relationship since. I won't get close to anyone. There's too much pain involved in relationships. . . . Sometimes I feel like I'm cheating myself, but sometimes I just say it's all for the best.

Thus, the coping strategy of remaining a single mother and moving on with parenting alone is perceived as the responsible course of action in violence-filled neighborhoods where the "streets are taking the men."

Teenage girls who have been physically and/or sexually abused in their childhood often speak of a teenage romance as the first loving relationship they have ever known. They seek approval, acceptance, and affection. Chiquita Gomez had been sexually and physically abused as a child. Her emotional state was very fragile. At age 16, she met a 19-year-old young man who became the center of her world. His attention and affection toward her meant everything. For the first time in her life, she really felt good about herself and thought she had something to live for; she had hope. They talked of being together forever.

Chiquita says she was never much of a student. She dropped out of high school in the ninth grade. Her relationship with her boyfriend gave her a reason to dress up, fix her hair, look pretty. Then Chiquita got pregnant. She wanted to have the child. Not only was she excited about starting her own new family with her boyfriend, but also she hoped it would get her out of an existing abusive family environment. It did not. The boyfriend left her for another girl. She was devastated. She gave birth to the child. Later, she fell off a third floor porch, was seriously injured, and hospitalized.

Now 18 and the mother of a 2-year-old daughter, Chiquita is fearful, untrusting, isolated, and living in a homeless shelter for teen mothers as she tries to figure out how to get through each day.

Not all never-married mothers are black or Hispanic inner-city teenagers. White teens, as well as white women in their 30s and 40s, are also raising their children alone if their expectations for a violence-free relationship cannot be met. Mary Magee became a single mother at age 45. She had been living with a man who became abusive during the pregnancy. She had the income, the resources, and, she believes, the good sense to leave the relationship. While it is a struggle juggling full-time employment, child care, and parenting an infant at midlife, she believes it is a lot safer than subjecting herself and the infant to potential bouts of abuse from the child's father.

In sum, the survival instinct motivates many single mothers, especially teenage mothers, to seek refuge from abusive partners. The coping strategy is to break off these relationships and live independently. It is not that teenage mothers are not choosing to marry, but that an abusive relationship—in marriage or not—is an irrational choice.

Impact on Children

The impact of domestic violence on children growing up in an abusive home cannot be underestimated. Children who experience family violence may act in an aggressive manner at home, in school, toward neighborhood children, animals, and adults. This behavior may also include destruction of property and theft. When these children become adolescents or adults, the violent behavior may be directed at their parents. When they enter adulthood they are more likely to batter their own partners or a spouse than are men who did not grow up in a violent home.[11]

In a crime scene reported again and again across the country, an adolescent boy is sought by police for allegedly killing his father. One such case currently capturing headlines is taking place in Rockland, Massachusetts, a working-class, suburban community outside of Boston. As the case unfolds, family members and the police substantiate the fact that the father had a history of violent behavior. Over the years, the mother repeatedly took out restraining orders against her former husband. She had divorced him six years earlier, claiming that he beat her. He spent six months in jail for violating one of the restraining orders. There was no restraining order in effect at the time of the shooting.

Family members say that the 17 year old was driven to shoot his father after suffering years of abuse and seeing his mother go through the same. On the night he was killed, prosecutors say the father had challenged his son to a fistfight, taunting him for being his mother's protector. The teenager's brothers say the boy felt forced to protect his younger brother and sister as well as his mother. The teenager reacted with behavior he learned from his father—use of physical violence to resolve a domestic crisis. Only this time the 17 year old was in possession of a .38-caliber revolver.[12]

A PUBLIC AND A PRIVATE ISSUE

In the last fifteen years, organizations with diverse constituencies such as the FBI, the American Medical Association, and the Bureau of National Affairs have all pointed out the devastating social, physical, and economic effects of domestic violence not only on individual women and children themselves, but also on the rest of society.

- The American Medical Association reports that violence committed by men against wives or girlfriends resulted in 100,000 days of hospitalization, almost 30,000 emergency room visits, and 40,000 visits to a physician *each* year.
- The nation's police spend approximately one-third of their time responding to domestic violence calls.
- Domestic violence costs U.S. companies between $3 and $5 billion annually from lost work time, increased health care costs, higher turnover rates, and lower productivity.[13]

Even though domestic violence continues to be one of the most frequently committed crimes in our country, it remains one of the most underreported. Findings from the National Crime Survey conducted from 1978 to 1982 revealed that once a woman was victimized by domestic violence, her risk of being victimized again was high. Close to half of all incidents of domestic violence against women were not reported to police. The most common reason given by women for not reporting domestic violence to police was that they considered the crime a private or personal matter. Fear of reprisal from the assailant was another reason. However, among the 52 percent of women who did bring the incident of domestic violence to the attention of police, one of the most common reasons given by these women for reporting the crime was to prevent future occurrences.

Victims are often deterred from calling police because previous calls were not thoroughly investigated and officials determined that the incident was only a family matter and not as important as other crimes. The National Crime Survey indicates that calling the police did seem to help prevent recurrences. An estimated 41 percent of married women assaulted by their husbands who *did not* call the police were subsequently assaulted again within an average six-month time period. For women who *did* call the police, 15 percent were reassaulted. Calling the police was therefore associated with 62 percent fewer subsequent assaults.[14]

Power and Control

As Mary Zagreb pointed out, a man who batters does not necessarily relinquish power and control with separation and divorce. State legislatures are becoming increasingly aware of the great potential for victim intimidation in cases of domestic violence and are passing laws to deal with this intimidation. "Stalker" laws, for example, attempt to protect victims, usually women, who are followed, harassed, and threatened over a period of time—often by ex-husbands or ex-boyfriends.

Often it is the combination of several forms of abuse that debilitate wives the most. For instance, a profile of the battering man shows him to be an intensely jealous person with an explosive temper. He will go to extreme lengths to isolate his partner from family, friends, and support systems in an effort to control where she goes, whom she sees, what she does. He insists on her dependency on him for money and survival, including taking her money and earnings or making her ask him for anything she needs. He may sabotage her employment, education, or other opportunities that facilitate her independence or sense of self-worth.

A man with a violence problem may exhibit drastic personality changes. He can be a loving husband and father at times and then periodically fly into explosive rages. He can be charming and pleasant to outsiders. This makes it hard for others to believe an abused woman when she may speak about her situation. A man who batters also blames other people and outside events for his own problems and behavior. He has a long-term pattern of avoiding the consequences of his behavior. This pattern limits his sense of personal responsibility for his destructiveness as well as suppresses any motivation for change. His partner becomes a surrogate punching bag.[15]

The profile of the woman who lives in this destructive environment can vary, but certain characteristics emerge. She acts as the buffer between her mate and the rest of the world and feels she must help him. When the battered woman says, "He needs me," she is right, in a sense. If he can continue to blame her for his problems and not have to deal with them himself, he does not have to accept the responsibility for his own behavior.

A battered woman accepts traditional male and female roles and accepts male dominance and superiority. She has an unshakable faith that things will improve, or she feels powerless—that there is absolutely nothing she can do about her situation. She accepts his reality, and she begins to doubt her own sanity. In this destructive environment, it is not surprising that women become passive, placating, easily dominated, and accept guilt even where there has been no wrongdoing. Many turn to alcohol or drugs to dull the pain. Others attempt suicide.[16]

Such realities make it extremely difficult for abused women to take the first step toward separation and divorce. The admonition to "just leave" doesn't work. They have no money, no resources, no transportation, no support systems, no self-esteem, and they do not believe they are capable of independent living. They also have the shelter and welfare of their children to be concerned about. Abusive behavior frequently escalates if they talk to their spouses about leaving the relationship. Many partners threaten to kill their wives at this time.[17] Others do kill. The anonymity of a battered women's shelter, of a homeless shelter, and of public assistance and a housing subsidy are often the only escape.

HOW DO WE RESPOND TO A VIOLENT SOCIETY?

In states around the country, judges, district attorneys, governmental officials, academic experts, and family advocates are seeking collaborative solutions to an increasingly violent society, especially among the young men. A 60 percent increase in homicides is being reported in some of the nation's larger cities, with police citing gangs, drugs, and domestic violence as the leading factors. In Massachusetts, for example, the state attorney general has declared domestic violence an epidemic that has reached crisis proportions for the victims, law enforcement, and the public. He remarks: "Without a dramatic change in societal attitudes, we will continue to have future generations who have grown up in families where violence is present, and society will continue to bear the burden of the human and fiscal costs resulting from that violence."

A recent Harvard School of Public Health research report names violence as the number one public health problem in Boston.[18] But the state legislature continues to drag its feet. Even legislators who strongly support victims of domestic violence are unclear how best to respond publicly. Some believe the problem of domestic violence is subsiding, that existing services are adequately addressing the crisis. Those who work directly with battered women, however, say more public support is necessary. They cite an increase in the number of women in abusive relationships who are seeking help in the state of Massachusetts alone. The critical issue is that inadequate funding for some programs may place women who are trying to leave their abusers in greater danger by encouraging them to get out of the abusive situation, but failing to provide enough protection for those who do.

The political debate with the legislature, according to the attorney general, is one of values: "Until everybody feels they are affected by the violence, we may not get the response we seek. I hope one day our values will be reflected in our appropriations priorities."

Protective Orders

The standard method of redress for victims of domestic violence is to obtain protective orders through the courts. They may be issued on an emergency basis for short-term protection for a few days when a victim can show there is a danger of immediate harm. After a contested hearing, a court may issue a longer term order of protection for prohibiting further abuse; prohibiting contact with the victim; excluding the offender from the victim's home, place of employment, or school; payment by the offender of spousal or child support, monetary compensation, or payment of alternative housing for the victim; or various other forms of relief. Offenders may also be required to participate in counseling, after which the charges against the offender may be dropped. In some states protective orders are valid for only three months, although the court may extend them if circumstances warrant it.

Women who go to court to get orders of protection are often shunted from court to court by judges and court personnel who would rather not be bothered with their cases. Criminal courts may insist that the crime is a domestic matter and does not belong in their courts. Some women become so demoralized by this process that they abandon seeking court protection.

Victim blaming is commonplace. Judges often ask men what the women did to provoke them. They often ask women what "suggestive" clothing they were wearing and why there are no visible bruises, even though injuries in domestic violence are more likely to be on the torso than on the extremities. Black women are especially disadvantaged by these inquiries because the bruises are not readily visible on their skin.

Some women find it difficult to get heard by the judge at all. A young mother from a middle-class suburb reports that it took her 2 1/2 years from the first charge of assault and battery against her husband until she got to court. The problem, as she saw it, was the "buddy" system among the policemen in her town: "The cops always let him go, unless it was the one woman cop. You just have to find one good cop. The District Attorney was good—a woman—who made him pay $500 as contribution towards my medical costs and go to counseling."

The need for protection can extend over many years. Mary Zagreb has lived in fear of domestic violence for ten years since her divorce. She explains:

There have been restraining orders out on my ex-husband on and off during the past ten years. He is still very angry at me. He still considers me his wife. He blames me for his problems, his drinking. There were periods when I didn't tell him where I lived. He pays child support and he sees his daughter every weekend. I don't think he would hurt her, but he could hurt me. I'm afraid of him and I avoid him, even now, ten years later.

District Court Judge Sydney Hanlon sees hundreds of battered women and their alleged batterers in her Dorchester, Massachusetts courtroom every year. On December 30, 1992, Judge Hanlon wrote:

We make another important mistake when we focus on solving the family violence problem only within the court and law enforcement systems. When we do that, we don't try anything else: we spend no state money for batterers' treatment and we aren't really sure what treatment, if any, works. There are more shelters for animals than there are for battered women, and a shelter is a very short-term solution—especially for a woman with children. We tolerate a society which is profoundly sexist and has violent homes in violent neighborhoods. Many of the men against whom

I issue restraining orders have never seen anyone solve a problem in a nonviolent way.[19]

The state judiciary is attempting to coordinate efforts in various departments to save lives. A statewide domestic violence recordkeeping system was implemented in September 1992 as part of that effort. The courts are now issuing approximately 1,000 restraining orders a week statewide. Each restraining order prohibits an identified potential batterer from going near the partner. On the positive side, only a very small percentage of these situations has ended in tragedy. On the negative side, it is shocking that in a presumed civilized society, as many as 1,000 court-ordered restraining orders a week should be required at all by one small state in the hope that women will not be abused.

SUMMARY

Domestic violence can be defined as physical, sexual, or psychological/emotional abuse used by a person to gain control and power over a victim. Ninety-five percent of all victims are women. Domestic violence has existed in traditional two-parent families for hundreds of years, with serious short- and long-term consequences for women, their children, and society. Abused women are increasingly seeking protection from violent behavior, and they may be forced to become single parents in order to escape abuse.

In increasing numbers, women are insisting on a violence-free domestic relationship. The single mothers in this study who were victims of domestic violence—and black urban teenage mothers in particular—are now taking a less romanticized view of intimate relationships. The cases reported here demonstrate how vulnerability exists long after a woman separates from her abuser, while the police and the courts have not yet found a way to protect her.

The political, economic, and social institutions of society are beginning to address the devastating effects of domestic violence on family life. Specialists are concerned about how to better counsel men who abuse women, but more importantly how to prevent domestic violence from happening in the first place. Law enforcement representatives and the courts express serious concern over the ineffectiveness of existing policies and practices to stem the tidal wave of abuse, a key factor in formation of single-parent families.

The overriding factor is that, despite research into the serious problem of violence against women in the family in the past fifteen years, there is a serious gap in our understanding and appreciation of the issue. Indeed, legal structures mirror the general societal view that wives are subordinate to and the property of husbands, to be disciplined or punished as husbands see fit. Developing responses to violence against women in the family will require accurate information on this societal dilemma. Shelters, police protection, and educational campaigns will be important short-term interventions. Ultimately, violence against women must be understood as a public community issue rooted in the subordination of women. The impacts of large-scale change will not be realized until fundamental shifts occur in the social and economic structures that maintain the inferior status of women in all spheres of life—within marriage and within the wider society.

NOTES

1. American Medical Association, "Domestic Violence: No Longer a Family Secret," in *Five Issues in American Health* (Chicago, 1991), p. 5.

2. National Victim Center, "Domestic Violence," INFOLINK, Vol. 1, No. 14, 1992; United Nations, *Violence Against Women in the Family*. (New York: United Nations, 1989).

3. The United Nations, *Women: Challenges in the Year 2000* (New York: United Nations Department of Public Information, 1991).

4. Simone de Beauvior, *The Second Sex*, ed. H. M. Parshley (New York: Knopf, 1953).

5. American Medical Association, "Domestic Violence: No Longer a Family Secret."

6. Susan Schechter and Lisa Gary, "Understanding and Empowering Battered Women," in *Abuse and Victimization Across the Life Span*, ed. M. A. Straus (Baltimore, Md.: Johns Hopkins University Press, 1988).

7. R. Gelles, *The Violent Home* (Beverly Hills, Calif.: Sage Publications, 1972).

8. Murray Straus and Richard J. Gelles, "Societal Change in Family Violence from 1975 to 1985 as Revealed by Two National Surveys," *Journal of Marriage and the Family* 48 (1986); and Murray Straus, "Wife Beating: How Common and Why?" *Victimology* 2 (1978).

9. Schechter and Gary, "Understanding and Empowering Battered Women"; United Nations, *Violence Against Women in the Family*, p. 22.

10. William Julius Wilson, *The Truly Disadvantaged: The Inner City, the Underclass, and Public Policy* (Chicago: University of Chicago Press, 1987).

11. Deborah Prothrow-Stith, *Deadly Consequences* (New York: HarperCollins Publishers, 1991); United Nations, *Violence Against Women in the Family*, p. 23.

12. Linda Gorov, "A Family Picture Framed by Violence," *The Boston Globe*, June 24, 1993, pp. 25 and 31.

13. American Medical Association, "Domestic Violence," p. 5; U.S. Department of Health and Human Services, "Family Violence: An Overview," Office of Human Development Services, Office of Policy, Planning and Legislation (Washington, D.C.: U.S. Government Printing Office, 1991); Prothrow-Stith, *Deadly Consequences*; National Victim Center, "Domestic Violence."

14. Patrick A. Langen and Christopher A. Innes, "Preventing Domestic Violence Against Women," Bureau of Justice Statistics, U.S. Department of Justice (Washington, D.C.: U.S. Government Printing Office, August 1986), NCJ-102037.

15. See R. Emerson Dobash and Russell Dobash, *Violence Against Wives: A Case Against the Patriarchy* (London: Open Books, 1980); and YMCA of Annapolis and Anne Arundel County, reprinted by permission of the Annapolis YMCA Women's Center.

16. Straus, ed., *Abuse and Victimization Across the Life Span*.

17. Edward W. Gondolf, *Battered Women As Survivors: An Alternative to Treating Learned Helplessness* (Lexington, Mass.: Lexington Books, 1988).

18. Report on Domestic Violence: A Commitment to Action, Harvard University School of Public Health, Boston, June 1993.

19. Sydney Hanlon, "Saving Battered Women," *The Boston Globe*, December 30, 1992.

—5—

The High Cost of Working

"I work my life then go to bed."

Ardeth Pierce, age 40

The general public is exposed to nightly television newscasters portending doom for the country whenever Census Bureau statistics indicate an increase in female-headed families. An assumption is made that such mothers will not work, only adding to the numbers on public welfare rolls. However, 77.9 percent of all mothers who head families with children between the ages of 6 and 17, and 58.8 percent of those with children under age 6 are currently working.[1] Their circumstances impose high costs on them. Yet despite the family costs, this level of employment among single parents reflects motivation, determination, and a serious commitment. Some single parents are not in the workforce because the costs of working and the barriers to entry are too high.

Two key employment issues confront single parents: (1) the high cost of working in relation to low wage expectations for most jobs women perform, and (2) the tug and pull between being good workers and good parents. Educated single mothers have entered the professions such as law, medicine, or management and can earn good wages. If they work the long hours required of many firms, these heads of household can have the resources to provide a decent standard of living for their families. But these fortunate women are the minority. Two-thirds of single mothers earn less than $20,000 a year, and 40 percent earn less than $10,000. Women with lower levels of education have low wage expectations and experience more barriers to employment that pays a family wage.[2] Self-sufficiency without good earning potential is nearly impossible.

This chapter first examines the consequences of low wages for individual single-parent families. Next, it identifies the barriers single mothers must face as they seek employment: availability of affordable housing and its proximity to good jobs; child care and health care; sexual harassment; the time and cost of education and training; and self-esteem and job readiness. Finally, societal attitudes toward women's changing roles, caregiving, and labor market participation are examined.

INCOME PACKAGING: WAGES ALONE ARE NOT ENOUGH

Most single mothers rely on their own earnings as their primary source of income, and they need and want these earnings to be adequate, regular, and reliable.[3] As a result, their job is the primary focus of their lives.

Although some single parents earn a "family" wage that can support a family in adequate housing and keep it healthy, most do not.[4] Single parents need an income "package" of wages *and* child support to keep a family stable; however, too few single parents receive both on a regular and reliable basis. Nonreceipt of regular and reliable wages, child support, or both, diminishes the family's economic base, which, in turn, adversely affects the family's living arrangements and psychological well-being.

Public assistance keeps the family living well below the poverty level, and its regulations create disincentives to work. Public assistance, however, represents regular and reliable income that also provides family health benefits. Working women find they need to "package" as many different sources of income as possible, both cash and in-kind, in order to meet a family's basic needs on their own.

Reliable Wages, Reliable Child Support

Education and skills help the single parent secure employment that offers regular and reliable wages. If adequate child support payments are received on a reliable basis and added to a mother's reliable wages, the income package can meet the family's basic needs. Paula Litchfield's case points out how this income packaging works to stabilize her family.

Paula is a college graduate who works full-time as an administrative assistant for a computer firm and earns $32,000 a year. Her paycheck is regular, and her company offers the health benefits she needs. Her ex-husband is employed and pays $800 a month in court-ordered child support to help meet the expenses of the couple's two children, ages 10 and 7. The child support is automatically deducted from his paycheck by his employer and sent directly to Paula. This procedure works efficiently for the family and for her ex-husband. It takes child support out of marital gamesmanship where withholding of child support by an ex-spouse is often used to express anger or to exact certain behaviors. The combination of both her own income and regular child support allows Paula and the children to live in a rented townhouse that meets their space requirements, is in safe and sanitary condition, is located in a safe neighborhood, and is in a suburb near her suburban job. She can meet her fixed, monthly housing expenses without threat of eviction. She also works productively because her income package is not in constant jeopardy.

Reliable Wages, Unreliable Child Support

In the past two decades, single mothers with a high school education entered or reentered the labor force in support positions, such as secretaries or clerk-typists. Such full-time positions generally offer reliable wages, but the amount received is usually insufficient to support a family. If child support from an absent parent is not received regularly in an amount needed to shelter the children, a single mother must spend time, energy, and money fighting her way through the court system to make sure the child support provision is enforced. Donna Jerome's experience is illustrative of this pattern.

Donna Jerome has been separated from her husband for eight months, and their divorce is in process. The couple has three children, ages 16, 14, and 4. Donna, who has a high school education, got a full-time job as a secretary in a large engineering firm that pays her $19,000 a year. A child support order is in effect for $800 a month, but her husband is already two months in arrears. She believes he is withholding child support to punish her for not immediately moving to cheaper housing when they separated.

Despite Donna's earnest efforts not to disrupt the family's living arrangements, she is close to losing her home, the centerpiece that keeps the family stable and frames her work-related decisions. Without child support payments, there is insufficient household income to meet the mortgage payments. Even if she can get the support order enforced through the courts, if her work hours are reduced to part-time, or if she is laid off, she will have insufficient resources to pay the mortgage.

Unstable Employment, No Child Support

Conventional wisdom unfairly holds that people who work the hardest earn the most money and that those who are poor simply do not work hard enough. Single mothers and others in low-wage jobs, however, *do* work long and hard, frequently at two low-wage jobs, and are still poor. The requirement to pay high rents or mortgages in the current housing market is frequently the driving force behind their labor-intensive lives that leaves the family house-poor and time-poor.

Ardeth Pierce, for example, works sixty hours a week outside the home at two jobs, yet she grosses only $17,280 a year. She was a full-time homemaker for twenty years when she and her husband split up. She receives no child support or alimony because her ex-husband is unemployed. She and her daughter live in a moderately priced two-bedroom apartment in the private rental market in a midsized city in the Northeast.

Ardeth got a full-time, entry-level, hourly wage secretarial job to support herself and her 14-year-old daughter. After taxes, deductions, and transportation expenses, she found to her dismay that she did not earn enough to pay the rent and utilities. She took a second job at minimum wage ($4.50 per hour) as a cashier in a retail store working some nights and every weekend. She is now able to pay her rent, utilities, and transportation.

The harsh reality for Ardeth has been the combination of entering the workforce in the middle of a stressful divorce, assuming the role of head-of-household, losing precious time with her teenage daughter who needs supervision and attention, losing her 16-year-old son who went to live with his father, and adjusting to a hard life filled only with long hours of low-wage work. It has affected her physical and mental health. Over the past two years, she lost 30 pounds owing to stress-related colitis and depression. She feels close to having a nervous breakdown, and remarks, "I work my life then go to bed."

BARRIERS TO EMPLOYMENT

From public pronouncements by politicians to coffee shop talk by average citizens, a common cry uttered about single mothers is, "Make them get a job! Married mothers are working now, why aren't they?" Single mothers *are* working, as Census Bureau and Department of Labor Statistics confirm.[5] Certain work/family tensions can impede the ability of all mothers to work and can affect their productivity and advancement on the job. However, there are certain barriers that become more difficult for single mothers to overcome because they are the sole support of their children. These barriers are: affordable housing and its proximity to good-paying jobs; access to affordable child care and health care; sexual harassment; the cost and time of education and training; self-esteem and job-readiness; stress and time of seeking child support; and conflicting societal attitudes about women's changing roles, caregiving, and labor force participation.

Housing Affordability, Location, and Work Opportunities

Employers have understood the important relationship between housing availability, geographic proximity, and employee productivity for over a century. In the early 1900s, manufacturing firms built company housing for their workers near their factories. Beginning in the 1950s and into the present day, firms have offered housing benefits packages for executives as incentives to employment. Such incentives can include low-interest mortgages; company-owned and -maintained single-family homes located in affluent suburban communities with good schools; paid housing renovation and redecorating budgets; or company-owned condominiums in major cities.

For most single parents today the housing/employment issue is housing affordability and geographic proximity to jobs that pay a living wage. The importance of this issue, however, is not well understood in the 1990s. Housing affordability means that the family's monthly rent or mortgage and utilities payment does not exceed 30 percent of their monthly income, a commonly used standard in mortgage lending institutions. When affordable housing is not available in areas that offer good employment opportunities, single parents are systematically excluded from this work because they can afford neither the housing that is nearby nor the cost of transportation to and from more affordable areas. The recent trend of corporations to relocate to urban fringe areas has intensified this housing/employment dilemma.

The shape and size of metropolitan areas have grown dramatically over the past two decades. Led by the relocation of large firms to peripheral areas called exurbs, the fringe areas are becoming new urban cores far removed from an area's inner city. In part, such corporate relocations are sited near middle-class housing developments in order to capture a much-needed educated workforce for the types of jobs required in the 1990s. While half of these newly created jobs are well paying, about half are local-serving and pay the least well. They have also been the most difficult jobs to fill.[6] This relocation trend to the extreme fringe will continue and could accelerate the post–World War II exodus of the middle class from center cities, leaving poorer city dwellers behind.

Housing affordable to the majority of single-parent families is not available in these new urban fringe job centers. In the 1980s, federal housing policy focused on tenant purchase of public housing units, even though public housing represents only 2 percent of the nation's housing stock. During the Reagan-Bush administrations, affordable housing programs were cut by 70 percent.[7] Many middle-and upper-income communities sought to increase affordable housing at the local level. But plans to construct housing affordable to lower- or moderate-income families brought intransigent resistance from residents through the NIMBY (not-in-my-backyard) syndrome. This resistance is usually codified through local zoning ordinances that prevent construction of housing for families who earn moderate or low wages. Projects targeted to low-income elderly, however, have been received with less resistance. When such affordable housing has been made available for lower- and moderate-income families, single-parent families have utilized them.[8]

Policy decisions that prevent construction of affordable family housing not only exclude single parents from the emerging job opportunities they seek, but they also deny access to valuable community resources such as good schools, quality public and private services, and supportive information networks—traditional stepping stones to improved social and economic status for most American families.

Access to Child Care, Elder Care, and Health Care

For decades, working women have sought workplace responses to family needs such as health and disability insurance, maternity leaves without loss of seniority, child care facilities, and provision for leave to care for ill family members.[9]

Child Care. The need for child care has been widely publicized as the nation has witnessed a dramatic increase in the number of mothers working outside the home. Quality, cost, and accessibility of child care are key issues.[10] Working mothers who earn the most money—regardless of marital status—pay the most for child care. They are also most likely to use private child care centers. Those who earn less primarily use informal arrangements and, to a lesser extent, publicly subsidized (more affordable) child care centers.[11] Those who earn modest incomes but have no access to either informal arrangements or good publicly subsidized centers rely on more costly private child care centers that soak up a high percentage of their total household incomes. Donna Jerome, for example, is paying about $500 per month, or 31 percent of her gross earnings, on child care for her 4-year-old daughter so that she can work full-time.

The growing number of working mothers with newborn children ensures that child care will be an increasingly important issue for years to come. By 1988, more than half of all women 18 to 44 years old who had a child under one year old were working, up from 31 percent in 1976.[12] This trend has serious implications for the growing need to develop quality, affordable, accessible child care services for infants, preschoolers, and school-age children.

Mothers earning low wages who have no access to low-cost, informal child care arrangements transition back and forth between low-wage employment and public welfare. One mother reported, "I'm not currently working because I can't afford child care. I used to work at an answering service 40 hours a week and I could bring my young daughter to work with me. Then management changed and I lost my job. I'm stuck on public welfare. It's a bad position because I can't work."

Another mother on public welfare was offered a job for $5 an hour selling movie tickets at night. The job offered no health benefits, and she could not earn enough to pay for child care. She stayed on welfare because she could keep her health benefits and avoid child care costs by being with her child full-time.

Mothers in midlevel management positions earning good incomes sometimes face the difficult dilemma of having to work long hours in order to keep their jobs at the risk of neglecting their children. In one current Massachusetts case, a manager who is a single parent is suing her former employer over this issue. Joanna Upton claims she was fired because she refused to work from 8:00 A.M. to 10:00 P.M. five days per week, plus Saturdays; she refused because doing so would have required her to neglect—more realistically, ignore—her son. She is alleging that the fundamental public policy of the state to protect and nurture families prohibits JWP/Businessland, her former employer, from forcing her to neglect her child in order to keep her job.

In her initial interview, the company confirmed its work hours to be from 8:15 A.M. to 5:30 P.M. with no lunch break and an after-hours meeting once or twice a month. Joanna arranged her child care for her son based on these hours plus her commuting time of an hour each way. She was the only single parent in the office. The requirements of the job changed right from the beginning, and even later as the job progressed.

Joanna did well and got along with her supervisor until she stayed home with her son one day when he was sick and she could not find a sitter. Soon after, the company merged with Businessland, and Joanna was told that the merger required her to work until 9:00 P.M. or 10:00 P.M. each evening and all day Saturdays for an indefinite period, at least several months. She explained that she would not be able to do that because of her responsibilities as a mother. She proposed working two or three nights and taking work home on the off nights and weekends. Her supervisor claimed to be aware of Joanna's situation, but two weeks later, Joanna was fired because she "was not a good fit" with the executive staff.[13]

Dual Dependent Care. The aging of the population often requires working women to attend to the needs of children and frail relatives at the same time. Women who head their own households experience numerous practical problems and fatigue from having to cope with dual dependent care (children and elders) issues, especially if there are no other adults in residence to provide a financial, emotional, and psychological buffer. The absence of appropriate institutional and community supports for the dual dependent care responsibilities of many employed single parents—and indeed for all working parents—results in increased absenteeism in the workplace and potential ill health for the caregiver.

Health Care. Single parents are one of the many constituencies seriously affected by the lack of a national health care policy. The elderly and the very poor qualify for federal and state health programs. Single mothers in the workplace only have family health coverage if their employer offers it at affordable rates. Large numbers of single parents who work part- and full-time do not have access to health benefits and are among the estimated 37 million uninsured Americans.[14] One 33-year-old widow could find only a part-time teaching job with no benefits. She is in particular need of family health benefits because her son is asthmatic, and the cost of self-insurance is very high. Between child care and health premiums it *costs* her $100 a month to work.

Sexual Harassment

Sexual harassment of women in the workplace is defined by the Equal Employment Opportunity Commission (EEOC) as

unwelcome sexual advances, requests for sexual favors and other verbal or physical conduct of a sexual nature when submission to such conduct is made either explicitly or implicitly a term or condition of an individual's employment; submission to or rejection of such conduct by an individual is used as the basis for employment decisions affecting the individual; or such conduct has the purpose or effect of unreasonably interfering with an individual's work performance or creating an intimidating, hostile, or offensive working environment.[15]

Numerous studies of sexual harassment of women in the workplace have determined that the incidence of sexual harassment was highest among women who were perceived to be "available" or "vulnerable." Available women were considered the single or divorced, Whereas the vulnerable were trainees, those holding jobs previously held by a man, or those with great dependence on their jobs such as single mothers.[16]

Researchers have shown that both victims and employers pay a high price. Victims quit their jobs or are fired, and most experience stress-related emotional and physical health problems.[17] Employers experience employee absenteeism, reduced productivity, increased medical costs, and turnover.

Lorraine Spivak's case points to sexual harassment as a power issue and of the direct economic consequences of being sexually harassed at work. Lorraine worked as a waitress on a part-time basis afternoons and nights. The owner of the restaurant offered her (and other waitresses he employed who were divorced, poor, and trying to support children alone) the chance to earn an extra $100 a week if she would have sexual relations with him on the weekends. If she complied, he would assign her preferred schedules to work on days and at hours when the tips would be the highest.

Waitresses who did not accept his sexual advances found themselves punished in monetary ways. First, he scheduled noncompliant waitresses to work only off-peak hours when tips would be low or nonexistent. Second, if a waitress did not pick up a customer's cash payment quickly enough on a busy night, the owner would take it off the table himself, allege the customer never paid it, and then dock the waitress's wages for the amount.

Lorraine seriously considered filing a formal complaint with the state commission against discrimination. She wanted the pattern of intimidation to end. But she also knew that if she filed a formal complaint, she would be immediately fired from her job. The time commitment to an investigative process and a hearing would be stressful on top of other stressful events in her life:

- Her child care arrangements were fraying. Finding more child care for something other than emergencies seemed complex and extravagant.
- Lorraine was trying to reduce her dependence on public welfare by participating in a welfare-to-work program. She needed to report all earnings with wage receipts at the welfare office on a monthly basis. Then the state calculated how

much money to deduct from her welfare check each month that was offset by earnings. She found this process to be time-consuming, complex, and bureaucratic because the office was located 10 miles away and she had no car.

- Her ex-husband was in arrears in child support payments, and a new court date to enforce the child support order was imminent. She feared retribution from him when he would be forced to appear in court.

- Her children had been sick and home from school lately. She was worried that the illness might advance into pneumonia.

On balance, these stresses wore her down. Lorraine decided not to file the sexual harassment complaint against her boss. Instead, she quit her waitressing job, with regrets at having to leave the other waitresses to cope with the problem. She believed that her boss's offensive and hostile actions should be revealed.

Lorraine's short-term solution was to transition back to public assistance as her only source of household income. This decision eliminated three of her five stresses: the unreliable child care problem, the sexual harassment, and the complicated reporting procedures to the welfare department. She then could focus time and attention on caring for her young children and pressing forward with the child support enforcement—both time consuming, stressful, and necessary commitments in their own right.

Child Support, Custody, and Visitation

Conflicts between mothers and fathers are not necessarily settled by a court decree that spells out terms of the legal divorce. Terms of the divorce decree pertaining to child support, custody, and visitation must be implemented "in the best interests of the child." Parents who differ as to what the best interests of the child are continue to experience stress. These differences often lead to time-consuming legal battles and court appearances, as we saw in Lorraine Spivak's case.

Stress of Child Support and Visitation. Conflict over tardy child support payments, a reduction in the amount of court-ordered child support, or nonreceipt of any agreed-upon child support are ongoing stressors. Mothers perceive that going back to court will aggravate the father, and thus increase the conflicts and level of stress between them. This makes contact between the parents more difficult, which is especially evident in willingness to accommodate a change in terms or conditions of visitation, or in civil behavior when the father picks up and drops off the children for visitation.

Sixty-four percent of the mothers with children under age 18 who participated in this study considered child support a stressful or very stressful aspect of their lives. Only 16 percent reported that they were comfortable or very comfortable with it.

Not surprisingly, 42 percent of those who found the child support issue stressful reported having unsatisfactory or very unsatisfactory relationships with the fathers of the children, and 14 percent reported having no relationship at all.

Caroline Hernandez explains how difficult it is to get over the emotional side of the divorce long after the legal side has been adjudicated:

Widows have it easier because they can go through the grieving process and get on with it. With divorce, you make a little progress in recovering, then your ex-husband appears or calls again and again with disputes about child support, visitation arrangements, or some complaint or other that picks off the scab that was healing the wound, and you bleed all over again. The problem is it never stops. It goes on for years until the children are grown.

Stress of Losing Custody. Mothers fear that fathers who are pulled back into court on child support matters may try to get even by suing for custody, even if they do not want it. Fathers who want custody but did not get it in the divorce may use a court appearance on child support as an opening to try again. Sonia Sager's situation illustrates how this can happen and what the consequences can be.

Sonia's husband John was a well-paid vice president of an international banking firm based in New York City when the couple divorced. She initiated the divorce, and he was bitter about it. She believes John never forgave her and wanted to punish her for hurting him.

John immediately remarried when the divorce was final. The court ordered him to pay $600 a month in child support for his 6-year-old son. Within four months, he stopped paying child support altogether. Sonia went back to court to enforce the order. Although it was enforced, the amount was reduced to $500 a month.

Sonia received no alimony because the court felt she was self-sufficient with a master's degree and work experience. She felt the property settlement was fair. She got a full-time job (to pay the lawyers, she says) and then bought a house in one of Connecticut's suburbs within commuting distance of her job in New York City.

Sonia and John had joint custody, so the child's time was divided between both parents. His remarriage created a traditional family form complete with a country house and two dogs. Sonia observed that her son was spending more and more time there. She also felt that her role as mother was immediately displaced by John's new wife who attended Charlie's school events and took Charlie's honors as her own. From Sonia's perspective, the new wife had no concept of her boundaries. Charlie seemed stressed and torn by the arrangement.

John sued for sole custody and won. Sonia found the judge was biased by the two-parent family structure:

With custody of Charlie, they closed the family circle. It never occurred to me that I could lose custody. There were no grounds. The court could find no grounds. . . . It said my 8-year-old son's wishes were more important than my 36 years of wisdom. The court didn't know what to do with me. I was in the way, disposable. The judge ignored the reality that Charlie and I could be a family too. The court didn't try to integrate me. The court discredited me. . . . It was form over substance. The image of being a family is more important than the emotional roots of family.

Sonia questions the morality of divorce and the gender bias that she experienced. For example, when she and her husband first separated, he immediately moved in with a woman. The court did not consider this in setting terms and conditions of visitation. Sonia's lawyer, however, advised her not even to date. Sonia observes, "Middle- and upper-middle class men have the intelligence and the means to manipulate the system to hurt their wives if they want retribution."

The role conflicts among the three people who assumed parenting roles in Charlie's life overwhelmed him. His mother has been cut out. She is not included in family milestones such as birthdays or Christmases. She does not get to meet his friends or attend parent/teacher conferences at school. Charlie will not see his mother on a regular basis as prescribed by the court. She still helps support him financially and plans to help with his college expenses in the future, per the court order in the divorce decree.

Sonia ceased officially to qualify as a single parent when she lost custody because she did not have a dependent child living with her. She is economically stable and her housing base is stable. She earns $90,000 a year as a company vice president, and she likes her work. Sonia would prefer to move back to New York City to be closer to her job. However, she continues to maintain the big house in the suburbs and commute just in case her son wants to return. Her personal adjustment is far from complete. The loss of custody and of the relationship with her son created an emotional crisis that destroyed Sonia's ability to deal with other relationships. She still has a profound sense of personal loss that will not go away.

The Cost and Time of Education and Training

Education and training are the primary requisites for jobs and advancement in fast-paced technical areas, manufacturing, management, or other emerging fields. Single parents aspire to employment that pays a living wage, career advancement, and a higher standard of living. Too often, they find they are resource-poor and time-poor in their ability to reach these goals. Obtaining child care arrangements and family health benefits are top priorities. If these needs can be met, single mothers can pay attention to the details of a job search, résumé writing, and school and educational loan applications. The clear tension, however, continues to be finding time also to meet parenting responsibilities.

Deborah Quinn, a 40-year-old divorced mother of four who is preparing to enter the workforce for the first time, explained her dilemma:

I want to work, but employers tell me I'm not equipped to work. I dropped out of high school to get married. In the last four years, I got my high school equivalency diploma (GED) and started at the community college. I took one course at a time, because that was all I could afford. I'm waiting now to see if I can get a Pell grant so I can take more courses. That's been the hardest thing, getting ready to be marketable. I've worked hard at home all these years taking care of my family, keeping the house clean, going without sleep. . . . Last year my son was ill with pneumonia and home from school 40 days. I stayed home to take care of him. How do you finish courses or keep a job when you're doing all this alone?

Educated women in the workforce encounter similar cost and time barriers. Even though Paula Litchfield receives regular child support payments, she still has neither the time nor the money to finish her education. Paula dropped out of her MBA program during her costly and disruptive divorce proceedings. She had completed one and one-half years of her part-time, three-year curriculum. She works full-time as an administrative assistant for a software company. Her $32,000 a year salary plus $800 a month in child support goes entirely to pay for living expenses and child care costs. There is nothing left to pay for tuition expenses for business school for her. Paula remarks:

Even if I could get money to pay for graduate education, there is no time anymore to attend school or study. I am doing all I can possibly do getting to and from work each day, working hard at what I do, and taking care of my girls alone. It is hard and exhausting. There's nothing left. I know I'm underemployed. But if I do anything else it would have to involve the girls so I could give them more time.

Thus high financial costs of education and training, in combination with the psychic costs of even less time with the children, create different decisions for those who want to be both good workers and good parents. Accommodations and trade-offs are made as single parents assess these costs in relation to their own individual resources of money, time, and stamina.

Self-Esteem and Job Readiness

Self-assurance and confidence in one's abilities are key elements for self-promotion in a competitive job market. Both men and women who experience marital dissolution express feelings of personal loss and instability regardless of educational attainment. Such jolts to self-esteem have adverse impacts on emotional well-being and often lead to social isolation from friends and support systems.

Workplace reentry is especially difficult for women who have been out of the workforce for some time. They are isolated from workplace-based supportive systems. If they frequently relocated to accommodate a husband's career, they may be physically and socially isolated not only from friends and family, but also from information about jobs.

Caroline Hernandez is struggling to regain a sense of self-worth. She has a master's degree and worked as a computer programmer before getting married. She has been at home full-time since the birth of her first child eight years ago. The family had just relocated to a new community in a new state where her husband accepted a job promotion. Within three months of their arrival, he moved out of the house and filed for divorce. She remarks:

Eventually I want to get back in my field, but for now I'm going to go back to work part-time in a toy store. I need to get my foot in the door, to recover, to talk to adults. The courts said, "You're an educated woman, so go back to work." But how do I do that with three small kids? I'm already working full-time taking care of them alone. I can't earn enough working part-time to pay for child care, but what can I do? I have to heal myself. . . . The woman across the street became a widow about the same time I was divorced. We're the same age. We were both grieving. Neighbors came to her with flowers, casseroles, offers of assistance. No one came to me with anything. They seemed to be saying if you're divorced there is something wrong with you. Then you start to believe it about yourself. It's very hard to recover when your feelings about yourself are rock bottom already, then reinforced by neighbors and friends who shun you.

Caroline needs personal support systems to help her regain confidence in herself and her own capabilities. She would like to move back to her home state near her large, supportive family where she knows she can get the close, personal acceptance she needs at this time. If she moves the children out of state, however, her ex-husband and his new wife will file for custody of the children on grounds that the move will deny the father proper visitation rights. She fears they would win—and judicial history concurs—because of their larger income and traditional family form.[18] She then would have lost everything. She feels isolated, threatened, powerless, and without choices.

Those who are socially isolated are often geographically and informationally isolated from access to jobs as well. The young, low-income single parents of color who live in central cities are at most risk. For decades, studies have pointed out the importance of job access to the probability of employment of urban youth.[19] Traditionally, access is defined in locational terms—that is, physical distance from available jobs. But a recent study found that urban youth also require informational access (access to knowledge about jobs) in addition to geographic proximity. It was found that social networks supply youth with jobs. Unemployment rates were significantly higher among black youths in cities where the Black poor were more socially isolated.[20]

SOCIETAL ATTITUDES TOWARD MOTHERS, CAREGIVING, AND WORK

American women receive "mixed" messages as to what their family roles should be and whether they should be in the workforce at all. First, some believe it is in a child's best interest for a mother to stay at home full-time in the child's early years of development and to be home when school-aged children return from school. On the other hand, if she must rely on public assistance to do this, a mother can be branded as lazy and living off the public trough.[21]

Second, some argue that women are needed in the workplace to fill gaps in certain sectors of the economy; women have followed the heed and entered the labor force in record numbers. But private firms and public policymakers have been slow to enact supportive child care, family leave policies, or education and training programs with child care provisions that would enable mothers to enter and retain labor force participation without undue hardship. When a single parent works the long hours demanded by her employer and spends less time caring for her children, some suggest she is a neglectful parent. If, instead, she works a shorter schedule for the same employer or requests time to care for an ill family member, she runs the risk of being characterized by her employer as "unreliable."

Third, access to an income gives women more independence in their relationships with men.[22] Such changes in role equity have unleashed a major societal backlash against women's growing independence.[23]

A historical view shows a separation of the private domain of family life from the public domain of the labor market. Women traditionally worked in the private domain of family. They raised children, and they cared for ill family members and the elderly. They washed, cooked, shopped, cleaned, scrubbed, and took time to relate to family members. With women taking full responsibility for domestic work, men were free to be involved in the public domain of the marketplace.[24]

In a market economy where value is measured in terms of money, low value is ascribed to a service that costs little, and no value is placed on a service given for nothing.[25] Thus, women's domestic work and caregiving in the home, for all its professed importance to child development, is devalued in the marketplace in large measure because it is a free service.

As women began to move into the public domain as wage earners, they quickly learned that family-related skills were neither respected nor valued. If their fourteen to sixteen hours a day of domestic work was so valuable to society, why were prospective employers telling them they had no experience? In effect, their work had no transferable value. Because she had performed the services for free, she had, in effect, "done nothing."

Donna Quinn's case illustrates the confusion that is felt when a mother's perception of her own worth as a caregiver is at odds with employers' and others' she now meets. What adds to the confusion is a message given that full-time motherhood is acceptable when a woman is married, but becomes unacceptable just as soon as she is divorced, when the children may need it most. Donna remarks:

No employer cares that I am skilled at taking care of sick kids, at keeping a house clean, at going without sleep . . . nobody cares about that. Nobody cares that you alone sit through dance recitals, discipline your kids, are there when they have asthma attacks at 2 in the morning. Now that I'm divorced, people say "Are you working yet?" I don't know, am I? You tell me. . . . Being a mother has no prestige whatsoever. Being a mother alone is even worse.

Educated women with previous work histories experience similar attitudes from employers when they move in and out of the workforce or reduce work hours when their children are young. One key issue is discontinuity of employment, and another is the limited value ascribed to volunteer work.

For example, Betsy Mullin was out of the workforce for only two years while her two children were babies. She had eight years of previous professional social work experience and a master's degree. During her two years as a full-time mother and homemaker, she did volunteer work at a juvenile jail counseling teenage offenders.

Betsy applied for a part-time position in the public sector as director of a new juvenile justice diversion program when her youngest child was 2 years old. The manager who interviewed her offered the job but at entry-level wages with no prorated benefits. Because she and her husband had recently separated, she needed more than entry-level wages for family needs. Moreover, she knew that she was worth more to the employer than an entry-level employee. Her educational and professional background exceeded job requirements.

The manager remained firm in his conviction. He replied, "But you haven't done anything for two years." From his perspective, being out of the paid labor market negated all of her previous employment history, and the value of her volunteer work, though precisely in the area of job skill being sought, was dismissed. Volunteer work was not paid work; therefore, it was not considered real work and was devalued in a market economy. Betsy did not take the job.

This pattern of leaving jobs, transitioning in and out of the labor market, or reducing work hours to care for small children reinforces the wage gap between men and women. In contrast, men more typically move up as they get more experience.[26]

SUMMARY

Women who head their own families want to work, and the majority are in the labor force, but they are torn by the desire to be good parents, too. Occupational segregation keeps many women employed in low-wage jobs. Wages from a mother's employment alone are usually insufficient to meet her family's basic needs. She requires the packaging of multiple sources of income that need to include regular and reliable receipt of child support in an amount sufficient to meet children's basic needs.

Barriers exist that make balancing work and family responsibilities very difficult for sole providers. These barriers include unavailability of affordable housing in geographic proximity to good jobs, access to affordable child care and health care, the time and cost of education and training, the effects of low self-esteem on job readiness, and sexual harassment in the workplace. Conflicting societal attitudes toward women's roles in the home and at work further complicate work/family decisions.

Millions of women who head their own families are working in spite of these obstacles, attesting to their motivation, perseverance, and diligence in coping with multiple stresses. For some mothers, the barriers are too high. In the final analysis, single parents have limited choices. They continue to walk a tightrope between the two worlds of work and family, even when there is no safety net.

NOTES

1. U.S. Department of Labor, Bureau of Labor Statistics, "Employment in Perspective: Women in the Labor Force," Report 822, Fourth Quarter (Washington, D.C.: U.S. Government Printing Office, 1991), Table A-18, p. 50.

2. Christopher Jencks, *Rethinking Social Policy: Race, Poverty and the Underclass* (Cambridge, Mass.: Harvard University Press, 1992).

3. Teresa Amott, "Working for Less: Single Mothers in the Workplace," in *Women As Single Parents: Confronting Institutional Barriers in the Courts, the Workplace and the Housing Market*, ed. Elizabeth A. Mulroy (Dover, Mass.: Auburn House Publishing Co., 1988), pp. 99–122.

4. U.S. Bureau of the Census, "Marital Status and Living Arrangements: March 1990," *Current Population Reports*, Series P-20, No. 450 (Washington, D.C.: U.S. Government Printing Office, 1991).

5. Ibid.

6. C. Leinberger, "Business Flees to the Urban Fringe," *The Nation* 255, No. 1 (1992).

7. Peter Dreier, "Bush to the Cities: Drop Dead," *The Progressive* 56, No. 7 (July 1992): 22.

8. Elizabeth A. Mulroy, "Mixed-Income Housing in Action," *Urban Land* 50, No. 5 (May 1991): 2–7.

9. S. Kamerman and A. Kahn, *The Responsive Workplace: Employers and a Changing Labor Force* (New York.: Columbia University Press, 1987).

10. J. Veum and P. Gleason, "Child Care: Arrangements and Costs," *Monthly Labor Review 114*, No. 10 (1991): 10–17.

11. Ibid.

12. Steve Rawlings, "Single Parents and Their Children," U.S. Bureau of the Census, "Studies in Marriage and the Family," *Current Population Reports*, Series P-23, No. 162 (Washington, D.C.: U.S. Government Printing Office, 1989), Figure 15.

13. *Joanna Upton vs. JWP Businessland.* Norfolk Superior Court, Civil Action 92–482.

14. Bradley Googins, *Work/Family Conflicts: Private Lives—Public Responses* (New York.: Auburn House Publishing Co., 1991).

15. D. E. Terpstra and D. D. Baker (1987) as quoted in Sally J. Kaplan, "Consequences of Sexual Harassment in the Workplace," *Affilia* 6, No. 3 (Fall 1991): 51–52.

16. Ibid., p. 52.

17. Ibid.

18. Lynn Hecht Schafran, "Gender Bias in the Courts," in *Women As Single Parents: Confronting Institutional Barriers in the Courts, the Workplace, and the Housing Market*, ed. Elizabeth A. Mulroy (Dover, Mass: Auburn House Publishing Co. 1988), pp. 39–72.

19. Alexander Polikoff, *Housing the Poor: The Case for Heroism* (Cambridge, Mass.: Ballinger Press, 1978).

20. Katherine O'Regan and John Quigley, "Labor Market Access and Labor Market Outcomes for Urban Youth," *Regional Science and Urban Economics*, Vol. 21, 1991, pp. 277–292.

21. Charles Murray, *Losing Ground* (New York: Basic Books, 1984).

22. Felicia Kornbluh, "Women, Work and Welfare in the '90s," *Social Policy* 21, No. 4 (Spring 1991): 23–39.

23. Susan Faludi, *Backlash: The Undeclared War Against American Women* (New York: Crown Publishing, 1991).

24. Hilary Land, "Time to Care," in *Women's Issues in Social Policy*, eds. Mavis MacLean and Duicie Groves (London: Routledge, 1991), p. 13.

25. Ibid., p. 7.

26. P. Loprest, "Gender Differences in Wage Growth and Job Mobility," *The American Economic Review* 87 (1992): 526–532.

—6—

Teen Mothers in Urban Poverty

"I never realized being on my own would be so hard."
Janice Brown, age 19

Teen mothers who live in poverty neighborhoods are the object of scrutiny, the subject of policy debate, and a unit of social concern. This chapter shows how the concentration of acutely poor female-headed families in poverty neighborhoods is a function of the interrelationship of multiple factors: the level of support and the role played by a single parent's family of origin and the father of her baby; the effects of federal and state housing and urban neighborhood policies; and the teen mother's personal coping abilities.

Bryan Roberts (1991) suggests that the distinction between coping and social mobility strategies is blurred for the urban poor. Coping strategies can be defined as organizing the family to get by in the short and medium term, while social mobility strategies refer to those decisions that have longer term beneficial effects: purchasing a home, getting an education to improve career prospects, or saving for a child's education. This chapter explains how the complexity of urban teen mothers' lives and key factors in the urban environment combine to generate a scramble for basic needs that lasts over time, making social mobility strategies difficult. Prolonged uncertainty creates family instability which demands a repertoire of coping skills to meet basic needs. Teen mothers with the fewest family supports and no access to quality affordable housing or to community-based resources have the most limited choices and may ultimately find themselves funneled into deteriorating neighborhoods with few chances of escape.

NEIGHBORHOOD POVERTY

A key factor in the analysis of contemporary urban problems is use of the terms *ghetto underclass* and *ghetto poverty*. These terms are often used interchangeably both to define geographic boundaries of neighborhoods and to characterize the behaviors of residents who live there. This is a complex problem because the concept of poverty itself is difficult to define.[1] Jargowsky and Bane (1990) suggest that there is confusion about several different concepts because they are often discussed simultaneously:

- Persistent poverty: individuals and families that remain poor for long periods of time, and perhaps pass poverty on to their offspring.
- Neighborhood poverty: spatially defined areas of high poverty, usually characterized by dilapidated housing stock or public housing and high levels of unemployment.
- Underclass poverty: defined in terms of attitudes and behavior, especially behavior that indicates deviance from social norms such as low attachment to the labor force, drug use and habitual criminal behavior, bearing children out of wedlock, and receipt of public assistance.[2]

Persistent poverty is defined in terms of time, neighborhood poverty is defined in terms of space, and underclass poverty is defined in terms of behavior. Therefore, single-mother families, high school dropouts, and public welfare recipients (and especially those with all three characteristics) who live in neighborhoods with unemployed men, drug addicts, and criminals also come to be associated with deviance from societal norms. At the center of the controversy is this question: Can the attributes of a shared space, that is, a neighborhood, imply shared behavioral attributes among all those individuals occupying that space?[3]

The definition of poverty used in this chapter is neighborhood poverty, because it focuses on the physical characteristics of housing and neighborhood environments.[4] At what point is an area considered a poverty neighborhood? Recent research suggests that a poverty rate of 30 percent used by Wilson (1987) or 40 percent used by Jargowsky and Bane (1990) corresponds to deteriorated housing conditions and ghetto poverty.[5]

In contrast to their suburban counterparts who do not want to move out of their communities, many urban single parents do want to relocate out of urban poverty to better housing and neighborhood environments which they believe exist in the suburbs or in smaller cities.[6] Two factors influence the quality of life for teen single mothers who live in inner cities: (1) relationships with and support from the family of origin and father of the baby, and (2) the likelihood they will end up living in neighborhood poverty.

Building on themes presented in Part I, this chapter examines these influences by examining their impact on the lives of four young women, all teen mothers, who live in different housing situations: the parental home, the private rental market, public housing, and a Section 8 subsidized apartment. Each case traces the role of families, of fathers of the babies, and of housing policies, regulations, and programs as factors influencing a single mother's housing choices. It also describes the demographic characteristics of the neighborhoods in which each woman lives. Case examples illustrate the diversity among teenage mothers and also depict urban life in transition in the 1990s.

ROLE OF MOTHER'S FAMILY AND OF FATHER OF THE BABY

In his State of the Union Address to Congress on January 25, 1994, even the president of the United States argued that teenage mothers should stay in their parents' homes, and not venture out themselves as heads of house holds maintained only by public welfare benefits. Indeed, the more sources of material and social supports a pregnant teen has from those closest to her, the more choices she has. The dilemma for so many, however, is that they either end up with few, if any, supports from those closest to them, or the sources of support, especially from fathers of the babies, are absent when they are needed most.

Many teenage mothers and their children do continue to live with their own families whenever possible. The Census Bureau considers them subfamilies in the household of others—not heads of households in their own right. However, a host of conditions that have nothing to do with receipt of public welfare may force a young woman out of the family home. For example, a new mother and her baby who stay on with a family already living in overcrowded conditions becomes the overcrowding "tipping point"; the mother and infant are asked to move out because their presence adds too much commotion and stress to an existing fragile family system. Particularly stressed are (1) parental remarriages which bring children from previous marriages into the same living arrangement, and (2) families of origin that live in public or subsidized housing for whom new household members violate terms of the lease and threaten eviction because of over-crowding.

Some parents are so angry at their teenage daughters who become pregnant that they disown them and force the girls to leave home in shame. Family violence such as physical, sexual, or emotional abuse within a pregnant teen's family also precipitates her leaving. She may be a victim herself, or she may leave to protect her child from abuse.

Marrying the father of the baby has been the traditional and desirable living arrangement encouraged by family and by the state, but those who have married and still end up as single parents explain that marriage alone is not enough. Love quickly sours in the face of a tough reality in urban poverty. Single mothers report that a young man's lack of steady income, dealing or doing drugs, and escalation of physical and emotional abuse as the pregnancy progresses cause them to seek independent living if they can find it.[7]

Whenever a teenage mother is on her own and becomes a head of household in the private rental market, she is severely disadvantaged by her low level of income. If she seeks public housing or a subsidized unit in a private development, she may be on a waiting list for years. If she is selected for tenancy, she may find a suitable unit in a safe neighborhood and become quickly stabilized. Or she may also end up in an unsafe public housing or other low-rent development located in a neighborhood filled with frightful drug-related violence. Or she can easily end up homeless—either as a never-married or as a separated or divorced mother.

The teenage single mother's youth further handicaps her. Not only is she likely to be low income, but she also has little or no experience as either a co-head or a head of household at a time when she is thrust into the housing market to find accommodation for herself and a child (or children) on her own. The acquisition of coping skills in completing a housing search in a hostile rental market, family budgeting, parenting, and home maintenance is limited by her inexperience. The combination of such structural and personal factors makes homelessness likely and movement out of the homeless shelter system to permanent housing very difficult.[8]

The four case examples presented next are of teen mothers who live in what we will call the Central City metropolitan area, but in a variety of living situations. Two live in "Mayfield," a close-in small city adjacent to Central City with a population of 28,710. One lives in Cabot, another close-in city with a population of 53,884. The last lives in an inner-city neighborhood of Central City itself. Central City has a population of over half a million people. The entire metropolitan area experienced job loss in manufacturing and population decline during the past two decades which precipitated a deterioration in the economic, social, and physical condition of many urban residential neighborhoods in older cities of the industrial Northeast.

LIFE IN THE PARENTAL HOME

Mayfield is one of many close-in small cities that form a ring around Central City, which buffers it from the suburbs. Historically a settlement for newcomers and immigrant populations, the city has recently experienced economic decline, physical deterioration, fiscal and political problems, and a decrease in population. It is the first city in its state since the Depression to be placed in state receivership.

Family Support/Violent Relationship

Eighteen-year-old Doreen Sheehan, a white mother of an infant, has lived in Mayfield all her life in the same two-family house. Her grandmother, who owns the house, lives upstairs, and Doreen, her 8-month-old baby, her parents, and four brothers and sisters share the downstairs four-bedroom unit.

Most houses in the neighborhood are two- and three-family properties mixed in between apartment buildings. Only 28 percent of the city's housing is owner-occupied, while 20 percent of all housing units have been declared substandard by the city. Thirty-five percent of neighborhood residents are minority, mostly Hispanics. Although the city's median family income is $29,039, 25 percent of residents in Doreen's neighborhood live in poverty. However, 68 percent of single mothers who live in this neighborhood live below the poverty line, that is, with incomes below $11,570 for a family of three. There is a 12 percent unemployment rate among males, but among Hispanics it is estimated to be 25 percent.[9]

When her mother found out Doreen was pregnant, she was very angry and disappointed and wanted her to leave. Her father, on the other hand, was very disappointed but said he did not want her to leave. One factor was the violent response from Bob, her 17-year-old boyfriend.

In the beginning, Doreen and Bob had what she considered a good, trusting relationship. However, when she got pregnant in what Doreen describes as sex against her will, Bob started treating her badly, withdrew, emotionally denied paternity, and went back to occasionally dating an old girlfriend. Bob's behavior became more angry and violent as the pregnancy progressed. He talked to her in a mean and nasty way, slapped and hit her, and threatened to punch her in the stomach.

After the baby was born, Doreen was faced with a serious income dilemma. First, she needed a source of income to help support herself and the baby, but she did not want any further contact with Bob at all because of his violence and involvement with drugs. If she applied for AFDC, the state would automatically seek Bob out to pay child support directly to the state. If he did pay, she expected he would seek visitation rights. The stress of continued, long-term contact with Bob through visitation and her fear of his violent reaction prompted Doreen to forego AFDC altogether as an income option.

Second, she could have dropped out of high school and gone to work, but she had been at the top of her class academically before she got pregnant and she still had some hopes and dreams left. With no source of income, she could not pay for an apartment on her own. Third, if her parents continued to support her and the baby, the best option she figured was to live at home and stay in school. Her parents were aware of how difficult it was for single mothers in the neighborhood to get by, and what dead-end, hopeless lives they seemed to have. They weighed the benefits and costs of letting Doreen stay at home or forcing her out. She and her parents finally negotiated the third option, but it has not been without great stress between her and her mother.

There were some tangible rewards in the end. In spite of the stresses caused by the unexpected pregnancy and the baby's birth, Doreen still managed to graduate from high school with a very good academic performance. This achievement, in combination with her family's low-income status, helped Doreen qualify for admission to a major, private, four-year university and a full tuition scholarship valued at about $16,000 a year. She is studying Education there now and is still living at home to make ends meet.

LIFE IN THE PRIVATE RENTAL MARKET

Four out of five mothers who head families alone live in the private rental market and juggle their low incomes with high housing costs. Given the expensive urban housing market, if public welfare is the only source of income, the amount is generally insufficient to afford market rents. Apartments will cost on average far more than their entire monthly income. The impact of this housing affordability squeeze can be observed in the quality of the unit a low-income mother can afford. According to HUD standards, evidence of a housing problem is measured by (1) affordability, (2) presence of overcrowding (number of persons per room), and (3) the physical condition of the unit. The situation of 19-year-old Janice Brown, a black mother of two, ages 3 years and 6 months, demonstrates the extent of housing problems on all three measures.

The Brink of Homelessness

Janice Brown also lives in the same Mayfield neighborhood as Doreen Sheehan, but Janice is on her own with her two children in a one-bedroom apartment and on the brink of homelessness. She is paying 83 percent of her monthly public welfare income for her one-bedroom apartment. She sleeps in the living room, and the children share the bedroom. She remarks:

My radiator's broke, it went down in March. I haven't had hot water in two months. It's rat infested in my ceiling and floor panels. It's a disaster. . . . The street I live on is okay, but drugs are a very serious problem on the weekends. You can see the piles of beer cans and little empty bottles of drugs in front of the houses.

What circumstances in Janice's family life caused her to resort to these living conditions? Did she have other choices? Although some families offer adequate space, resources, and healthy relationships for a young mother and her child, not all families of origin offer a suitable living situation. Other options are needed to protect her health and safety. Janice's situation is one example. She had been in foster care for four years. One night, at age 15, she was taken to the emergency room of City Hospital "for acting crazy—suicidal and things." She was sent to a psychiatric hospital where she was treated for four months.

Janice describes a childhood filled with fear, instability, and sexual abuse. She remarks:

It was total hell. There were problems all around me. I was raped when I was 8, 11, and 13. . . . It happened in my own house. It was the uncle of my mother's husband. He got real mad at my mother for something. Said "If I can't get you I'll get your daughter." So that's how he got back at her. He raped me. . . . There was no one to fall back on. Those times in the mental hospital were the happiest moments in my life, because I felt just so relaxed and cared for.

The state Department of Social Services took Janice into protective care on grounds of child abuse and placed her in a foster home. Vulnerable and insecure, she got involved with an older man, had her first baby, but remained in the care of a foster family until she turned 18.

Interactive Effects of Program Regulations

Janice married the father of her baby and they had a second child, but marriage alone did not make an appreciable difference in their lives. They could not make ends meet on his on-again, off-again employment, and they separated. Janice found that she was better off on AFDC not because the amount of income was more but because it was received on a regular and reliable basis. Janice retained a good relationship with the father of her children, and he came to see them regularly. He gave her about $50 a week to help with the children's expenses to supplement her monthly AFDC check of $579.

Then, the Department of Public Welfare actively sought to enforce child support, and her economic position quickly deteriorated. Regulations determined that he would pay the welfare department $120 per month, out of which Janice would get only $50, and the state would keep the balance as repayment on her welfare benefit. This reduced Janice's monthly income by $150 per month. This child support enforcement procedure angered her husband because he wanted Janice and the children to get the full, though modest, amount, not the state. He took off, and she does not know where he is. Now neither she nor the state get any child support money from the children's father, and the children have lost the personal relationship with their father.

Her biggest disappointment was that marriage did not turn out to be a happy, secure arrangement, and that her husband abandoned her and the children. She reflects, "I was so young, I just fell in love with him. I don't know why. I didn't have my head right. I think I was blinded by love."

Despite this very bleak period and a history of abuse and abandonment, Janice still has hope and long-term goals for her family that require moving out of the inner city:

I'm looking for a safer, better environment for my kids . . . waiting for a Section 8 certificate. I don't want to live in the public housing projects. That's where people die, where they break into your house. As a woman with two daughters I don't want them to get hit by a stray bullet, get snatched up or something, I couldn't live with that headache. Some people take this easy way out. I'd rather not.

Use of Housing and Social Support Services

Janice views the apartment in Mayfield as a temporary stopping point toward a long-range goal of a better life and is utilizing housing, social service, educational, and legal resources to improve her situation. First, she applied for public housing in nine suburbs and small cities where she is on waiting lists. The largest Housing Authority in the metropolitan area currently reports that there are 23,000 families on the waiting list for conventional public housing unit and 13,000 on the Section 8 list.[10] Janice hopes there will be fewer people on the suburban waiting lists. The Section 8 program that Janice seeks first requires her to stay on the waiting list for at least two to five years and then allows her the opportunity to search for an apartment. It does not guarantee a housing unit as in the conventional public housing program.

Second, Janice continues to look for a cheaper apartment with a landlord who will rent to a single mother with children and on AFDC. Given the reduced supply of affordable housing in the private rental market, this is an unlikely but hopeful course of action. Third, she receives help from a legal assistance corporation to help protect her from eviction at her present apartment while she looks for an alternative. Fourth, she is in psychological counseling to help her cope with the deep wounds left from the multiple traumas of her childhood. Fifth, she continues to further her own education in a GED (graduate equivalency degree) high school equivalency program. She is well aware that she needs a high school education and attends full-time in order to improve her life-chances and the future well-being of her children.

Janice is resilient as she continues to persevere to be a good parent, to complete her education, and to improve her living conditions. Her coping skills are notable considering the severity of traumatic life crises she has already endured and the multiple environmental stressors from her current housing problems.

LIFE IN PUBLIC HOUSING

The advantage of public housing is a consistently affordable rent—30 percent of income—but the disadvantage for urban teenage mothers can be its location in unsafe surroundings. A safe location near jobs facilitates social mobility; a physically isolated, unsafe location does not. Many young mothers are trying to finish high school through GED programs or to attend job-training programs that require them to come and go at various hours of the day and evening. The unsafe housing and neighborhood environments of many older projects are leaving them scared and isolated from social programs targeted to assist them. This creates a barrier to completing their education and training programs because they barricade themselves inside their housing units at sunset.

Public housing is the domain of local housing authorities who, from the beginning, decided where developments should be located. In large, older cities such as New York, Boston, and Chicago, most of the original projects were sited in areas where the poor already lived. Newer projects, especially in the West, were often scattered in different locations to avoid concentration of the poor.

The Funnel-Effect into Neighborhood Poverty

The housing situation of 20-year-old Patsy Young and her 2-year-old son illustrates (1) the relationship between housing and social supports, (2) how opportunities are limited by public housing location, and (3) how fear of crime and neighborhood violence restrict what residents can do and where they can go.

Patsy lives as head of the household in Webster Gardens, a large public housing project built in clusters of three-story buildings with 365 family units. She pays only $120 per month for rent and utilities, which is about 30 percent of her adjusted $446 monthly welfare grant.

Webster Gardens is located in an inner-city neighborhood in Central City and was built in an area that is now racially segregated and poor. Ninety-eight percent of neighborhood residents are racial minorities, mostly black. The median income for all families in this city is $34,377, compared to $20,119 in the Webster Gardens census tract. Because the female-headed family is the predominant family form in the Webster Gardens area (60 percent of all family households), and their median family income is $11,707 (only $5,075 for families on public assistance), the neighborhood itself is very low-income; 36.6 percent of all persons in this neighborhood live in poverty. This is more than twice the ratio for all families citywide.[11]

Webster Gardens is considered one of the most dangerous public housing projects in the city; Patsy does not live there by choice. It was the housing of last resort in a year-long search involving no parental support, restrictive public and subsidized housing program regulations, and no locational or geographic choice.

Her path to these accommodations began when she was kicked out of her mother's and stepfather's apartment at age 16. Her mother, an AFDC recipient and a reported heavy drinker, remarried, and hoped that a two-parent family form and the increased income would improve the living situation for herself, Patsy, and a brother. The stepfather and Patsy, however, did not get along. There were charges that he sexually abused Patsy. This new living arrangement proved to be an unsafe one, and Patsy could not stay.

From then on Patsy's housing history was framed by federal and state housing regulations pertaining to public or subsidized programs. In the beginning she moved in with her boyfriend Bill's family in a mixed-income rental development. The family was low-income and lived in a subsidized apartment in a development that had mostly market-rate apartments—a very nice housing and neighborhood environment. Patsy felt that members of Bill's family were warm, accepting, and supportive, unlike her family of origin. They helped her learn how to do basic things like pay bills and get a checking account.

Patsy was very upset when she got pregnant. She considered having an abortion but felt that it was not morally the right thing to do. She remarks, "I had the choice to have the baby or not have it. It was my choice; therefore it's my responsibility, whether the father helps or not." Marriage to Bill, who was then also 18, was not an option for economic reasons. He was in a full-time GED program through Jobs for Youth and was not employed. There was no way he could earn enough money to support her unless he dropped out of school and worked. This short-term strategy would preclude the couple's longer term goals that could only be realized if Bill finished his education and then went directly into the job-training program.

Patsy was proud of Bill's long-term goals and his short-term actions to finish school and get job training. She felt it was *very hard* for young black men to follow this path today because it meant standing up against very strong peer pressure, such as the magnetic pull of gang affiliation and the lure of large sums of easy drug money. But Bill did not do drugs, and this was extremely important to her. Patsy was sure Bill would financially support her and the baby just as soon as he finished his programs and then got a job.

A critical housing shift occurred after the baby was born. Patsy was required to move out so that Bill's family would not be evicted for breaking lease terms pertaining to overcrowding of their subsidized apartment. The property management firm that regulated leases determined that Patsy and the baby's presence in Bill's parents' apartment officially created over-crowded conditions as defined by federal housing quality standards of one person per room. The purpose of enforcing federal housing regulations is to improve the housing quality of low-income tenants so that their apartments are affordable, not overcrowded, and in safe physical condition. Even though Patsy wanted to stay on with Bill's family, and they were happy to have her and the baby as well, she was forced to move out or else Bill's entire family could have been evicted.

Patsy's options were limited: she could not afford an unsubsidized apartment on her welfare benefit. She could not have moved back into her mother's and stepfather's apartment because that living arrangement had been an abusive one from which she sought relief when she first ran away. In effect, she was forced into a head-of-household living arrangement through a combination of public program regulations and personal circumstances.

Patsy took two clear actions. First, she applied for her own subsidized apartment in the same housing development in which Bill's family lived. However, her application for tenancy was rejected by the property management firm. Second, she applied for city public housing and was put on a waiting list. Eventually, she was given a choice between two public housing projects, both located *an hour away* from Bill's family (her support system) or anywhere else she needed to go, such as school. She finally chose one because it was a little closer to Bill's family, but she did not consider this a rational housing choice. She was forced to move from a safe, secure neighborhood to an unsafe, distant place in a very bad neighborhood because the rent was affordable. She has only lived there for two months but wants to transfer to another project.

The Transportation Dilemma

Patsy and other young, urban single mothers face the same complex dilemma as their suburban, divorced counterparts in their difficulties juggling home/school/work/child care responsibilities on their own. The key struggle for Patsy and other urban single mothers is the geographic distance that must be traveled on public transportation to accomplish what most teens generally consider a simple task—going to high school. Because Patsy dropped out of school in the tenth grade, she is trying to get back on her feet by attending a full-time, year-round high school equivalency program. The school projects that at her pace of learning it will take Patsy two years to complete her degree. This service-intensive program is located at a social service agency on the other side of the city to which there is no direct public transportation from her home. Patsy describes her commute:

To get to school by 9:30 A.M. I get up at 6, get myself ready, pack up the baby's gear for the day and my school materials. I get the baby up, feed him, and leave the house by 7:30 A.M. First I have to take the baby to day care before I go to school. I walk with the baby to the bus stop across from Webster Park and pick up bus 22. I take that, then get off and transfer to bus 16 which takes me to State Ave. where I get off and take the baby to the YWCA day care center. Then it's 8:05. I wait for bus 8 which takes me to Mudley Station. There's a school bus that picks several of us up and takes us across town to school. If I miss the school bus because of bad connections I have to catch bus 66. I get off and transfer to bus 57 which drops me at the bottom of the hill. Then I walk up the hill to school.

When school is out at 2:00 P.M. she reverses the entire route and gets home at 5:00 exhausted. She is coping with this daily routine in the summer but is cautious about what it will be like in the cold, snowy winter months. She hopes she can do it, despite the long stretches of walking the route requires.

Unsafe Neighborhoods

Patsy is very concerned about her unsafe neighborhood because it restricts her from school programs or activities scheduled in the evenings. First, she is afraid to walk alone from the bus stop to her apartment in the project after dark. She does not know any of her neighbors, although tenants are mostly single mothers of color and their families. When she finally gets home, she bolts the door and draws the blinds. Someone was shot and killed outside her apartment window recently. Illegal drugs are a very serious problem. Patsy comments, "It's a terrible, unsafe neighborhood. I'm worried about stray bullets crashing through the window. Once I come home from school I don't come back out for nothing. I don't talk to no one. One night I got home late and was too scared to go into my own building."

Second, she is worried about her son's safety and well-being if she switches him to the day care center located at the public housing project. This action would greatly shorten her commute time and make completing school more feasible. However, Patsy wants to be a good parent and is torn between doing what would make her life more efficient versus what is in her son's best interests. She is concerned about his physical safety amidst the illegal drugs, the gangs, and the shootings. She comments:

He is so happy in his day care center, and taking him out would be bad for his development. His child care center at the YWCA is one of the best in the city. If he's at day care in the housing project all day while I'm far away at school I couldn't protect him. I'd worry all day. Now I go to school with peace of mind.

She wishes she could afford to live closer to school, but median rents in that section of the city are now $780 for a two-bedroom apartment, and there are no more federal or state subsidies for rent relief.[12] She wishes she had a choice. But she does not. Patsy's short- and long-term coping strategies are linked together. Patsy and Bill continue to have a supportive, loving relationship and hope eventually to marry. With no family economic support to draw on, they decided to postpone both living together and marriage until Bill finishes his education and has a job. In the interim, Patsy is mobilizing all available resources and working hard herself to properly care for her child on a daily basis in a hostile housing and neighborhood environment. She hopes that her efforts will eventually lead to long-term benefits for the whole family—if they all survive.

Patsy lives in neighborhood poverty, but is she a member of the ghetto underclass? If the stresses of neighborhood poverty force her to drop out of school in order to protect her child full-time, will she be stereotyped with deviant ghetto underclass behaviors of welfare status, detachment from the labor force, high school dropout, child out of wedlock, living off the public trough, and isolated from mainstream opportunity for upward mobility? How can she escape poverty from this starting point with so many barriers to overcome?

LESSONS FROM HOUSING SECURITY WITH A SECTION 8 SUBSIDY

A very different outcome was realized by 19-year-old Ada Montana, who, in a two-year time span, went from life in poverty in a homeless shelter to life as a full-time, summer employment trainee with Digital Corporation earning $7.10 an hour. She was homeless because her family of origin lived 3,000 miles away and the father of her child, in her words, "took off."

The linchpin in her turnaround was success in utilizing a Section 8 housing subsidy to rent a two-bedroom apartment in Cabot, a small, close-in city near both Central City and Mayfield. Settlement into a physically adequate apartment for which her portion of the rent was $100 a month then gave Ada, an Hispanic, the opportunity to pay attention to other things. She reentered high school and once there was selected to participate in a special mentoring program between the high school and the Digital Corporation that offered income, child care subsidies, and transportation to the work site.

Income Packaging

Ada's level of family well-being improved because her total family income increased. She was allowed to keep her public welfare check of $446 a month in addition to the $800 a month summer earnings, while the state subsidized all the child care costs for her 2-year-old son. The combination of subsidized rent, subsidized child care, and a $1,246 gross monthly income offered her income security—at least for the summer. She went back to living on only $446 a month in September when school started and the job training ended, although the goal is transition to full-time employment at program completion.

Housing and Neighborhood Satisfaction

From Ada's perspective, her Cabot neighborhood is a very good place to live. She is satisfied with her overall housing conditions. The houses in the neighborhood are well maintained, and the streets are clean and free of litter. She feels that the people who live on her block are good neighbors, but even more important, she feels that it is safe to walk alone in the neighborhood at night.

The demographics of her Cabot neighborhood suggest socioeconomic and racial diversity. The median family income in her neighborhood is $36,801, while citywide it is $42,099. Even though 40 percent of families in her neighborhood are headed by a female, only 6 percent of all families live in poverty. Moreover, 19 percent of neighborhood residents are racial minorities, with more Asians than blacks or Hispanics.[13]

Role of Housing Search Assistance

Ada did not succeed in finding a suitable unit in this neighborhood on her own. As a homeless, AFDC recipient she was eligible for housing search services, a program through which housing advocates assist homeless women with children to navigate the complex process of finding suitable rental apartments and willing landlords.[14] The Cabot Housing Authority, through which Ada received her Section 8 certificate, reports that use of both Section 8 subsidies and public housing in Cabot by single mothers at a critical time in their lives was a key factor that stabilized legions of women who eventually moved on to professional careers and independent lives.[15]

HOUSING POLICY, FAMILY SUPPORT, AND SELF-SUFFICIENCY

Teen mothers are a diverse group, but they share a similar problem: their unmet basic needs far outstrip the ability of many already-poor families to meet these needs. They are limited by their youth, inexperience, and youthful boyfriends who most often do not stay the course with adequate economic and social supports for long-term relationships or parenthood. Doreen had a family safety net that her parents agreed to use, but Janice and Ada did not. While Patsy's family of origin did not offer a family safety net, Bill's parents did. Yet federal regulations prohibited her from using the physical resources of their safe housing and neighborhood environment, which, in turn, separated her from their social and economic support systems as well.

All four teenage mothers experienced unplanned pregnancies. They also shared the value that abortion was the wrong choice for them. Once pregnant, giving birth was perceived as the responsible thing to do. Therefore, they turned to public resources for varying levels of assistance to meet some aspects of their basic needs to fill the gap left by families and partners. Currently, Doreen's baby is on Medicaid for health coverage. Janice receives public assistance, Medicaid for herself and the children, and food stamps. Patsy and Ada receive public assistance, Medicaid, food stamps, and housing subsidy.

The location of Ada's housing subsidy in a culturally diverse neighborhood of a small city in a metropolitan area that does not have concentrations of racially segregated housing is the critical factor that gave Ada social mobility, safety and security, and community-based access to educational, and ultimately to employment, resources. An important point is that she did not secure this housing on her own, but needed assistance that helped to break through barriers in the housing market. Patsy, on the other hand, lives in concentrated poverty where educational and support services are not community-based, and thus are more difficult to access and utilize.

All four young women exhibit motivation to help themselves. They lead complex lives in basic efforts to complete school and take proper care of their children. Janice and Patsy demonstrate perseverance in searching for better housing conditions. They even demonstrate hopefulness when living amidst neighborhood poverty, a condition beyond the imagination of those who have not endured it.

SUMMARY

Teen mothers most disadvantaged in their housing are those with the lowest incomes and fewest family supports because they have the fewest choices. Separated, divorced, and never-married mothers need housing security to hold together a complex and fragile array of related needs: educational and employment opportunities, child care, transportation, and personal supports. Yet they experience residential mobility that can funnel them into neighborhoods of concentrated poverty from which escape is difficult. They are not there by choice; they are there because they have no other options.

The poverty of many urban neighborhoods, tentative—often traumatic—relationships with families of origin, and abandonment by many teen fathers unable to economically support a family on a regular basis make a teen mother's search for safe, affordable basic shelter a difficult one for her to accomplish alone, and much harder than she ever anticipated. Those who turn to social and legal services to facilitate the housing search may be more successful in finding a subsidized unit in a neighborhood of their choice. In turn, family stabilization can take place in a community that is more likely to offer physical safety, and educational and employment opportunities.

NOTES

1. For an in-depth discussion, see, for example, William Julius Wilson, *The Truly Disadvantaged: The Inner City, the Underclass, and Public Policy* (Chicago: University of Chicago Press, 1987); Mark Alan Hughes, "Misspeaking Truth to Power: A Geographical Perspective on the 'Underclass' Fallacy," *Economic Geography* 65, No. 3 (July 1989): 187–207; Mark Alan Hughes, "Concentrated Deviance and the 'Underclass' Hypothesis," *Journal of Policy Analysis and Management* 8 (1989): 274–281; F. R. Ricketts and I. Sawhill, "Defining and Measuring the Underclass," *Journal of Policy Analysis and Management* 7 (1988): 316–325.

2. Paul A. Jargowsky and Mary Jo Bane, "Neighborhood Poverty: Basic Questions," working paper series, Malcolm Wiener Center for Social Policy, John F. Kennedy School of Government, Harvard University, March 2, 1990, p. 2.

3. Mark Alan Hughes, "Misspeaking Truth to Power," p. 190.

4. Census tracts are used here as proxy for neighborhoods. Census tracts are areas defined by the U.S. Census Bureau, typically containing about 2,000 to 8,000 people. In a densely settled neighborhood, a census tract may be the size of four or five city blocks. This definition is used by W. J. Wilson (1987) and by Paul Jargowsky and Mary Jo Bane (1990).

5. Jargowsky and Bane, "Neighborhood Poverty," pp. 9–10.

6. Elizabeth A. Mulroy, "The Search for Affordable Housing," in *Women as Single Parents: Confronting Institutional Barriers in the Courts, the Workplace, and the Housing Market*, ed. Elizabeth A. Mulroy (Dover, Mass.: Auburn House Publishing Co., 1988).

7. See Chapter 4 for a detailed examination of the impacts of domestic violence on single mothers.

8. Terry Lane and Elizabeth Mulroy, "Analysis of the REACH Program, 1988–1992: A Study of an Emergency Housing Program for Homeless Pregnant Women," prepared for Crittenton Hastings House, Boston, 1993.

    9. Demographic data from U.S. Census Bureau, 1990 Summary Tape Files 1 and 3.

    10. Lane and Mulroy, "Analysis of the REACH Program," p. 28.

    11. Sources of demographic data are from the 1990 U.S. Census, Summary File Tapes 1 and 3.

    12. Cushing N. Dolbeare, *Out of Reach, Why Everyday People Can't Find Affordable Housing* (Washington, D.C.: Low Income Housing Information Service, September 1991).

    13. U.S. Census Bureau 1990 Summary File Tapes 1 and 3.

    14. See Barbara Sard, "Housing the Homeless Through Expanding Access to Existing Housing Subsidies," *New England Journal of Public Policy*, Special Issue on New England and Beyond (Spring/Summer 1992): 187–201.

    15. Interview with Jack Daly, Malden Housing Authority, January 28, 1994.

—7—

The New Uprooted: Housing and Divorce

I've moved three times in four years since separating from my husband. Each time I've tried to get cheaper rent. I'm now paying three-quarters of my income on housing and child care, trying to get a nice place for the kids and near my job. If this landlord raises my rent I'll be evicted because I can't pay any more.

Charlene Fabiani, age 35

Housing problems of single parents are not limited to inner cities. Suburban single-parent families also experience residential instability and housing problems. This chapter examines how separated and divorced single mothers cope with the effects of the housing crisis in the resettlement of their families. Coping strategies here, as in Chapter 6, refer to short- and medium-term actions, whereas social mobility strategies refer to longer term actions and expectations.[1]

Roberts (1991) suggests that "The more formalized the urban environment and the more stabilized the labor market and its rules, the more likely it is that households will be differentiated by whether or not they have long-term social mobility strategies or shorter term coping strategies."[2] This chapter examines how housing affordability, location, and labor market concerns affect the ability of suburban single parents to engage in longer term, social mobility strategies.

The set of decisions single parents make over the long term to ensure their family's shelter needs are also dependent on several personal characteristics: their income, race, marital status, age, living arrangements, number of chil-

dren, employment status, location of employment, and whether they own or
rent their housing at the time they become single parents. For example,
divorced women are more likely to be homeowners during marriage and
attempt to stay in a similar permanent housing situation after the divorce.
Single mothers who live in urban poverty, especially never-married teens,
seek basic shelter from public and subsidized housing, but in the absence of
an adequate supply they remain cost-burdened in the private rental market.
Widows, who are usually older, experience the least housing stress. They more
often live in their own homes and have accumulated assets and insurance. The
separated and divorced are starting over, while the young, never-married are
trying to start from a disadvantaged position. This chapter first examines how
disposition of the marital home is a critical factor in both short- and long-term
family stability. Second, lessons from housing security of the 1970s are
explained in order to compare and contrast factors that help stabilize divorced
families and facilitate long-term social mobility decisions.

WHO MOVES? WHO STAYS?

Housing options available to those women who are separated and divorced
are constrained by the disposition of the family home in the divorce settlement,
and their amount and sources of income after marital dissolution. Homes are
generally considered marital property. Cars, clothing, furnishings, businesses,
savings, investments, and houses acquired during the marriage are the property of both spouses. In some states, all marital property must be divided in
half at the time of the divorce. Other states divide property according to an
"equitable distribution" that gives a judge power to determine who gets what
in assets and debts regardless of whose name is on the deed, bankbook, or
loan application. Evidence suggests that women are often shortchanged in
division of marital property. Many judges perceive women's unpaid work in
the home to be an inconsequential contribution to acquisition of marital assets
or to her husband's career advancement.

Who gets to stay in the marital home has critical implications for single
mothers and their children. At the time of separation, one spouse usually
leaves the matrimonial home and the other stays. But studies show that over
time both spouses have much more mobility than one might expect, and the
key reason is affordability.[3]

DISPLACEMENT AND MOBILITY

Residential mobility after separation and divorce is a critical housing issue. Displacement occurs when any household is required to move because of circumstances beyond its control. The growth of one-parent families in the suburbs raises concern about suburban displacement that forces relocation to central cities because of a lack of affordable housing for families generally in the suburbs. In one study those not displaced who remained in the marital home were fathers with custody and widows.[4]

Many women are awarded the marital home in property settlements where sufficient assets have been accumulated that can be divided equitably. The problem arises when the marital home is the only marital asset, and unfortunately, in most marriages this is the case.

One approach to housing and divorce is for both partners to retain financial interest in the marital home after divorce, but the mother retains the sole and exclusive right to its use for a specified number of years, or until the youngest child turns 18, at which time the home is sold and the proceeds are divided.

Couples who recently divorced and had to divide their assets in the declining real estate market of the late 1980s and early 1990s were at an additional disadvantage. The consequences of economic change, of job layoffs, and of the housing crisis had serious consequences for such families. The following case examples spotlight three families who were all homeowners during marriage. They illustrate a range of options available to them at marital dissolution pertaining to disposition of the marital home and the consequences of the decisions that were made.

Sale of Marital Home

The first case example points out the effect of economic decline in the Northeast on one family's level of economic security and marital situation. The Pierce family had lived a traditional life in terms of roles and responsibilities for twenty-one years. Peter Pierce worked outside the home to provide economic support, while Ardeth Pierce was a homemaker taking care of the family. In 1987, at the peak of the real estate boom in the Northeast, she and her husband Peter sold a home in which they had substantial equity and purchased a new suburban house for $200,000. It was a major step up for them.

Shortly thereafter, her husband lost his job because of a company merger, a loss that had profound and long-term effects on their family structure as well as its well-being. The couple could not afford the costs of their new home. Loans were taken out, but the bills piled up. The strain was overwhelming. The relationship eventually broke down from the burden of economic stressors, and they filed for divorce.

As part of the 1991 property settlement, they sold their house in a depressed real estate market for $169,000. When all debts were paid, there were no marital assets to divide.

Ardeth's first concern was how to get immediate income to feed, clothe, and shelter herself and her 14-year-old daughter. Ardeth received no child support or alimony because her husband was unemployed. She thought he collected unemployment insurance, participated in a federally funded job retraining program, and might potentially work again. Ardeth, however, had no employment history. Her options for income were limited to either public welfare or low-wage employment. She chose to work and entered the labor force for the first time at age 43.

On her income, Ardeth could not afford to rent an apartment but there were no other adult family or household members to earn additional wages. Therefore, she took a second job herself. She is now working 60 hours a week at two low-wage jobs earning a total of only $17,280 a year in order to support her housing costs of $800 a month for a two-bedroom apartment (considered a moderate rental in her area according to HUD guidelines) that shelters herself and her daughter. In effect, the entire family is a middle-class casualty of economic restructuring.

Father Stays in Marital Home

A factor that puts women and children at a disadvantage in property division is that judges often find a way to keep the husband's business intact, but require sale of the family home—in effect the wife's business. Some men are awarded the family home if they built it themselves, if their business is based there, or if money from their parents was used for its purchase.

In Charlene and Abe Fabiani's situation, Abe stayed in the suburban marital home after separation. Abe Fabiani successfully argued before the judge that because his landscaping business was attached to the house, he needed to stay on to guarantee the success of his business and thus ensure his ability to pay adequate child support. Charlene and the two children, ages 2 and 4, moved out.

The economic recession of the early 1990s adversely affected Charlene's husband's business, and he had difficulty paying monthly $800 child support payments on a regular basis. Four years later, the couple was still

separated, and some elements of the property settlement remained unre-
solved. In the meantime, Charlene and the two children had moved three
times within two suburban communities. Each move happened because a
landlord increased the rent to a level she could not afford to pay. She had
to move or be evicted.

Charlene's housing options were constrained by several factors that
became interrelated: joint custody of the children; a need for employment
but a lack of job skills; need for quality, affordable child care near home
and a work setting; need for an affordable rent near her husband's house in
the suburbs; reduced supply of government-subsidized suburban rental
housing.

Role of Custody Agreement. The key constraining influence on her
housing search was the limited locational or geographic distance she could
consider due to the joint custody arrangement. Charlene was required—and
also committed—to remain in this nice town where her husband lived
because the children spend half of the week with their father and the other
half with her. In effect, the children moved back and forth between each
parent's house every few days. Therefore, their school and day care arrangements had to be close to their father's house too. This community of choice
had a population of 21,500, of which 98.3 percent was white. Over three-
quarters of all housing units were owner-occupied.[5]

Simultaneous to embarking on a housing search, Charlene, like Ardeth
Pierce above, needed enough income to pay for a moderately priced
apartment. The $800 in monthly child support was received on an irregular
basis that depended on how Abe's business was doing in difficult economic
times.

Role of Economic Supports and Housing Subsidy. Charlene's choice was
to stay at home full-time with her two children because they were so young.
Therefore, she sought to augment her income through public welfare, but
she did not qualify. Receipt of child support—even irregularly—put her
over the income threshold set in eligibility requirements of federal/state
public welfare regulations.

Charlene then made a series of decisions to get herself economically
stable and housed on her own; she sought part-time employment. First, to
help transition her into the job market, she entered a federally funded
job-training program that included a child care subsidy. She successfully
completed the program, learned clerical skills, and then got a part-time job
in a lawyer's office. She has no health insurance or other benefits, however.

Second, Charlene found a good child care provider in the same community.
Third, a housing search in that community resulted in finding a three-bedroom

house to rent. The house was a winterized beach cottage a stone's throw from the ocean renting at $800 per month, a moderate price in this town. What a find, and what a nice environment for the children. Charlene saw the pieces of her life coming together and the family stabilized at last.

Within a few months it became apparent to Charlene that she did not have sufficient income to pay both her housing and day care costs and still have any money left for food, medical expenses (she had no health insurance), and other family neccessities. Charlene's gross earnings from her part-time, hourly wage job were $768 per month. When combined with $800 in child support (in the months it was received), her total monthly income was $1,568. Her rent alone was taking 51 percent of her monthly income, and child care costs (even with a state subsidy) were $340 per month, leaving only $428 for food, car expenses, clothing, medical costs, and other necessities for a family of three. She needed more income to make ends meet.

The next key decision she made was to apply for public and subsidized housing in her community in an effort to reduce her housing costs to an affordable level. Charlene's total annual income of $18,816—in relation to her family size in her region of the country (about 34 percent of the $55,524 median income of all other families in her town)—qualified her for a federal Section 8 housing subsidy program. Under the program, she would pay 30 percent of her income for rent, and the federal government would pay the balance directly to the landlord. She was on a waiting list for the program because there were so few subsidized units available for families in her area; nearly all the federal and state low-income housing programs in her community had been built exclusively for the elderly.

Eventually, Charlene's application came to the top of the Section 8 waiting list, and she got a certificate of eligibility to search for a unit in the private rental market through this housing subsidy program. The final outcome of her housing search, however, shocked her. She embarked on the housing search with great expectations. Charlene thought this would be the answer to her housing cost burdens. But soon she had to face reality: she could not find one landlord in the area to which she was restricted who would rent an apartment or a house to her with the subsidy. There were multiple reasons.

- Per HUD regulations, she could only rent a three-bedroom place because of the age and sex of her children. She could not find a vacant three-bedroom apartment in the suburbs anywhere at all.

- She found three-bedroom houses for rent, but landlords were asking more than the HUD-approved $970 rent limit in this increasingly well-to-do community.

- When she did find a three-bedroom house at that rent level or below, it could not pass the housing quality inspection standards HUD required, such as two electrical outlets per room, handrail on the front steps, and so on. Most of the houses were old because the community itself was old. Many houses had been remodeled and updated over the years and seemed adequate to the local folks and to her—but not to HUD.

- Landlords refused to participate in what they thought would involve government red tape.

At the end of the designated sixty-day search period, Charlene was required to return the certificate for housing subsidy unused. She was devastated. She was unable to use this only remaining federal housing program not because she did not try hard enough, but because the program itself was impossible for her to utilize in the suburbs. A combination of factors in the private housing market, as well as government program regulations themselves, hindered her ability to reduce her rent burden through the Section 8 program.

Charlene's landlord did raise the rent to $850 a month, an amount she could not pay. This forced Charlene to move out. With no place to go on her own, she temporarily moved in with relatives. Eventually, she found an apartment for $450 a month about 20 miles away in a working-class community. She relocated there because the price was right, but there was a geographic downside. Charlene had to travel much farther to her low-wage, part-time, clerical job in a marginally adequate car. It is unlikely that this arrangement will meet a cost/benefit test where benefits outweigh costs even in the short term. Moreover, the children are displaced not only from another home but also from their school, day care arrangement, neighborhood, and friends. They also bear the burden of adjusting to a more complicated joint custody arrangement.

Mother and Children Stay in Marital Home

Many mothers seek to stay in the marital home to keep the children stable, but this decision requires adequate postmarital income to pay the mortgage and to maintain the home. Donna Jerome's housing circumstance illustrates how difficult it is to maintain the marital home when mortgages are high from mid-1980s purchase prices and child support is not received in a regular and reliable manner. She stayed in the suburban marital home so that the children could remain in their safe neighborhood, in the same schools, near friends, and in a community where after-school activities and part-time jobs would be available for her two teenagers.

Donna reentered the workforce on a full-time basis after her husband moved out. She chose her employment primarily because it was only ten minutes from her home and six minutes from a suitable child care center for her 4-year-old daughter. This location-based home/employment/child care triangle reduced commuting costs and time, and provided her more time for routine as well as emergency parenting.

Role of Wages and Child Support. This carefully orchestrated plan had started to fall apart after only eight months because Donna could not afford to maintain her home without receiving a combination of wages and child support on a reliable basis, and child support had stopped. Donna remarked:

I vowed to keep the house. As soon as my husband left he said, "Move out to an apartment." But apartments in this area are also expensive. And what would happen to my two teenagers and four-year old growing up in an apartment building? I lived my whole life to get this house. I'm going to do everything in my power to keep it. If I give up the house I'll probably never get another one.

Despite Donna's earnest efforts not to disrupt her children's living arrangements, she was nearly displaced from her marital home. Without child support payments, there were insufficient earnings to meet the first mortgage payment. Separated for only eight months and not yet divorced, Donna could not count on regular receipt of child support, creating a forced move from the marital home. If her work hours were reduced to part-time or if she was laid off, her ability to pay the mortgage would be further jeopardized, even if she could get court-ordered child support.

Only half of all single mothers receive child support, and only half of those receive the amount due. When child support is paid by absent parents, the support most often arrives in the early phase of marital dissolution and is reduced or stopped over time.[6]

Moving Decisions. Donna considered moving to cheaper housing and pondered how that choice would benefit her situation. Certain location costs and employment-related costs were anticipated. First, most rental housing in her old, midsized manufacturing city was located in the central city where median rents for a two-bedroom apartment were about $750. Second, the size of her family and its gender makeup required her to rent at least a three-bedroom apartment in which her two girls (ages 16 and 4) would have to share a room. An apartment of this size would cost even more, if she could find a three-bedroom apartment at all.

Third, advertised jobs for secretarial positions (including her own) were located primarily in the opposite direction—out of the central city—at large engineering and high-tech firms that populated the suburban fringe along the region's interstate highway. There was no public transportation from the central city to these suburban fringe jobs. A relocation to cheaper housing away from her present location would fracture her already fragile suburban-based support network.

Fourth, a move to the inner city would add safety and school quality issues to her list of housing and neighborhood concerns. If she did not feel safe in her neighborhood after dark, it would restrict the hours she felt she could go to and from work. If her children were not living and playing in a safe neighborhood environment while she was at work, she would feel compelled to stay at home in order to monitor the children's activities and ensure their safety and well-being. Her 14-year-old son and 16-year-old daughter gave her the greatest worry in a prospective move to the central city because of known drug and gang activity. The highest cost would be if Donna were not able to put together a home/job/child care package in order to retain her present or any employment.

These three cases point to the role of changing sources and amounts of family economic supports after marital dissolution and its impact on housing affordability and stability for single-parent families. The role of both fathers' and mothers' employment and income levels, the absent parent's ability and willingness to pay adequate child support, and use of the marital home are fundamental issues in postmarital stability for children. In addition, the high costs of homeownership and of rental housing in the 1990s, the lack of affordable rental housing in the suburbs, and the inability to use the Section 8 housing subsidy in the suburbs all precipitate residential mobility, even when mothers make decisions to enter the labor force in hopes of earning enough to stabilize the family on their own. In sum, single mothers need adequate economic and social resources in order to (1) afford basic housing, and (2) parent well while they are moving back into the workforce and while the children are adjusting to changes in living arrangements.

LESSONS FROM HOUSING SECURITY IN THE 1970s

Much of the current public debate on single-parent families and their economic and housing situations is based on remembrances of an era before the impact of economic change and the housing crisis of the 1980s took hold. As recently as 1980, divorcing couples faced a very different set of social and economic forces, and their outcomes were decidedly different. When receipt of the marital home was combined with other support elements in the divorce, displacement was prevented, in part, because the cost of housing was so much less expensive.

The following section contrasts decision points and outcomes for single-parent families in the suburbs when the following elements are considered and provided for: (1) a realistic appraisal of housing costs, (2) receipt of regular and reliable child support that covers the cost of housing the family, and (3) a woman's earnings from employment near her home. The story of Bonnie Kamm is presented to illustrate how the family stabilization process can be ensured when all these elements are in place.

Bonnie and Phil Kamm were divorced in 1976 when the children were 5 and 7. In the property settlement, Bonnie received the marital home and Phil got the vacation house at the beach and the cash. She and the children remained in the home because it was affordable to do so then. Phil paid child support on a regular and reliable basis, although it did not cover all of the children's basic needs. He also paid the mortgage on the marital home directly to the mortgage holder. The couple originally purchased their house in the early 1970s for about $32,000; so the mortgage and interest rate on the loan were low.

After spending about six months trying to get over her intense anger toward her husband for walking out on the family, Bonnie got a job outside the home. She had some college education but never finished her degree. There were very few job opportunities for women in the suburbs in the mid-1970s.[7] Most male heads of households in Elmwood and other suburbs drove or took the train into the city to work about 25 miles away. This would be too difficult for her, she thought, because it would entail complex child care arrangements. Over the years, she had a series of clerical jobs in the surrounding area that did not pay much, but they were all she could get.

Even though Bonnie owned the house and Phil paid the mortgage, Bonnie's wages alone could not begin to cover all housing costs that still included property taxes, utilities, and maintenance costs. However, when she combined her low wages with child support that was received on a regular and reliable basis, the family remained stable in the marital home and never had to move. Phil also kept up contact with the children after the divorce and remained a significant person in their lives.

Residential stability in the town of Elmwood has given the family security, safety, and opportunity. The community, with a population of 17,000, is an affluent residential suburb of national historic significance in the Northeast. Ninety-three percent of the residents are white. Elmwood has always had strict zoning laws that require single-family homes to be built on at least one-half acre of land. Seventy-eight percent of all housing is owner occupied. The environment is picture-book serene—quiet, peaceful, and well-kept. Air and streets are clean, and there is lots of open space. Her children could ride bikes everywhere without fear for their personal safety. Bonnie is not aware of any drug problems in the community. A tastefully designed shopping center offers all the basic needs. There are no neon signs, no bars, no congestion. Both children spent their entire twelve years of public education in the same school system. Bonnie believes they got an excellent education. They are now in college and doing well.

By 1991, the property taxes skyrocketed to $3,500 even though the house needs repairs and a fresh coat of paint. As a result of the housing crisis in the 1980s, the home increased in market value; it was recently assessed for $310,000. Now at age 51 Bonnie works full time at an hourly wage job, but her gross earnings are only about $16,500 annually. Her housing security enables her to stay put in a community where the median household income is now $69,917, while the median family income is over $80,000.[8] She is on her own and does not plan to move. Nowadays she could not afford to.

Comparisons and Contrasts

Bonnie and Phil Kamm's situation illustrates that even fifteen years ago in a very different housing market, housing costs far outstripped the average woman's earnings potential. In order to keep the family stable in the marital home, several sources of income were needed. The father's role in payment of regular child support and of housing support in an amount adequate to keep the family in the marital home was necessary in addition to the mother's earnings in order to provide long-term residential stability for the children.

When compared to the case examples of displacement from the marital home in the 1990s presented earlier in the chapter, a clear theme emerges. Suburban single mothers in the 1990s experience downward social mobility because of reduced housing options at far higher cost, little appreciable improvement in women's wage expectations, and irregular payment of child support. Frequent residential mobility in search of more affordable housing unwittingly becomes a downward spiral that carries single-parent families to lower quality accommodation with each move. The lack of affordable family rental and homeownership options in the suburbs is a clear missing link for those families who need and want to remain in their own neighborhoods and communities in the aftermath of separation and divorce.

SUMMARY

Affordable apartments and homeownership opportunities are fundamental needs of separated and divorced mothers who were homeowners during marriage. They seek housing located in a safe, secure neighborhood environment near support systems and employment opportunities that pay a living wage.

The physical, social, economic, and psychological significance of housing profoundly affects how and where a family can live. Certain key housing decisions are made individually by a single mother and her ex-spouse. Such decisions, however, are circumscribed by community decisions that include (1) events in the private housing market that are guided by economic decisions of banks, lending institutions, real estate developers, and city policymakers, (2) policy shifts at the federal and state levels that help to determine the supply of affordable housing, housing program regulations, and eligibility thresholds of income transfer programs such as AFDC, (3) local suburban zoning decisions that exclude affordable rental and home-ownership opportunities, and (4) decisions of judges in property settlements pertaining to disposition of the family home.

Divorced and separated single parents who were homeowners during marriage have become the new uprooted because they experience residential mobility that can spiral the family downward into lower quality housing and neighborhood environments with each move. It is nearly impossible for low-wage single mothers to stop the downward spiral on their incomes alone because the costs of housing are so high. Therefore, the housing crisis has adversely affected homeowners and former homeowners because there are now few housing options they can afford at a time that their total family income has been drastically reduced.

NOTES

1. Bryan R. Roberts, "Household Coping Strategies and Urban Poverty in a Comparative Perspective," in *Urban Life in Transition, Urban Affairs Annual Reviews 39*, eds. M. Gottdiener and Chris G. Pickvance (Newbury Park, Calif.: Sage Publications, 1991), p. 139.

2. Ibid., p. 139.

3. For example, see Martin Rein et al., "The Impact of Family Change on Housing Careers," unpublished report prepared for the Department of Housing and Urban Development by the Joint Center for Urban Studies, Cambridge, Mass., 1980; Susan Bartlett, "Residential Mobility and Housing Choices for Single-Parent Mothers," unpublished paper, Joint Center for Urban Studies, Cambridge,

Mass., 1980; Elizabeth A. Mulroy, "The Search for Affordable Housing," *Women As Single Parents: Confronting Institutional Barriers in the Courts, the Workplace, and the Housing Market*, ed. Elizabeth A. Mulroy (Dover, Mass.: Auburn House Publishing Co., 1988), pp. 123–163; Frances Wasoff and Rebecca Dobash, "Moving the Family: Changing Housing Circumstances After Divorce," *Housing and Divorce*, Studies in Housing No. 4, ed. Peter Symon Center for Housing Research, University of Glasgow, Scotland, 1990, pp. 139–166.

4. Rein et al., "The Impact of Family Change."

5. Source of demographic data is U.S. Census Bureau 1990, Summary Tape Files 1 and 3.

6. Lynn Hecht Schafran, "Gender Bias in the Courts," *Women As Single Parents: Confronting Institutional Barriers in the Courts, the Workplace, and the Housing Market*, ed. Elizabeth A. Mulroy (Dover, Mass.: Auburn Housing Publishing Co., 1988), pp. 39–72.

7. Dolores Hayden, *Redesigning the American Dream: The Future of Housing, Work and Family Life* (New York: W. W. Norton, 1984).

8. Demographic data from the U.S. Census Bureau 1990, Summary Tape Files 1 and 3.

Part III

Transition and Stabilization

The final part offers prescriptions for transitioning one-parent families from the instability described in Part II to a stable state. Chapter 8 draws on accounts from divorced and separated mothers who made individual decisions regarding residential mobility that ultimately led to a more stable family situation. This chapter offers several examples of stable living arrangements for one-parent families. Chapter 9, the final chapter, recommends societal-level changes that are responsive to the basic needs of one-parent families. Social policy implications are drawn with a focus on improved housing and community development policies to meet basic needs. The chapter argues that national urban policy *is* family policy; that evolution of a caring society will guide development of urban policy into humane cities for all economically marginal families with children. Specific recommendations to strengthen single-parent families in the urban environment are suggested.

—8—

Family Restructuring after Separation and Divorce

Profound changes in the labor market, the housing market, and social policies—and the continuing revolution in how work will be conducted in the global economy of the 2000s—have created a vastly different environment for one-parent families to face today than the environment of merely fifteen years ago.

The previous chapters examined how women of diverse ages and circumstances struggle to meet basic family needs in the context of a changing environment. The chapters highlighted the interdependence of decisions made by individual women with those made by other persons and by societal institutions outside their sphere of control:

- The actions of fathers and the decisions of courts regarding property settlements and child support orders.

- Labor market decisions of firms; that is, where to locate new businesses, what worker categories to eliminate, what work/family policies to offer.

- Public-sector policies regarding the labor market, income maintenance, subsidized housing, subsidized child care, public education, employment, and training.

- Private landlord actions to obtain a fair market rent, and public community decisions to include or exclude affordable housing.

- The actions of ex-spouses and partners, of community law enforcement, and decisions of the courts regarding domestic violence.

This chapter focuses on individual and collective actions mothers can take to bring a family to greater stability. Three phases of family adjustment after marital dissolution (divorce or separation) are discussed, considering three key areas of adjustment: (1) changes in living arrangements, (2) restructuring family roles and responsibilities, and (3) seeking support for personal adjustment.

THREE STAGES OF FAMILY STABILIZATION

Divorce does not fit neatly into theoretical models of life-cycle development. Students of family relations find that discussion about one-parent families is usually appended in a textbook that treats single-parent families as a deviation from the norm. McGoldrick (1989) and Brown (1989), however, have developed a model of family development after marital dissolution that we will use for our analysis.[1]

Their outline suggests that a family passes through three distinct stages or phases of development in marital dissolution: (1) the Aftermath, (2) the Realignment, and (3) Stabilization.

The *Aftermath* is a state of crisis immediately after a couple separates. It is called Aftermath because it can be as turbulent as recovering from a natural disaster. Elements in the Aftermath are coping with financial hardship, parenting dilemmas, and social relationships (primarily isolation and feelings of abandonment).

Realignment is the transitional state. It involves interacting with environmental forces such as public and private agencies; adjusting family roles and responsibilities within the family; and assertively taking steps to improve personal adjustment through participation in support groups, formal or informal association with other single parents, and dating. According to Brown (1989), the Realignment phase generally lasts two or three years.[2]

The *Stabilization* phase includes achieving economic security through either remarriage or a good job if a woman remains single and attaining parenting skills with authority over her children.[3]

The scope and complexity of issues presented in the previous chapters suggest that events in the Aftermath of relationship breakdown make this stage a very long and bumpy one that takes *far* longer to navigate than is commonly realized. The environmental complexity in the 1990s impedes family realignment, keeping families in an ongoing unstable state. The instability of housing arrangements and fluctuations in levels of income and sources of economic support cause swings in and out of poverty. The length of time it takes to process a legal divorce, establish housing security, and obtain an economic base keep a family in a prolonged state of crisis for years.

A prolonged state of crisis postpones attention to internal family relationships and the development of the coping skills necessary for all family members who experience a major life transition. Women and children who are victims of domestic violence are particularly disadvantaged by these characteristics of the Aftermath. They are coping with multiple crises at the same time with the fewest financial resources and social supports.

Women do take individual and collective actions to shift a family toward Realignment. Many women reach Stabilization and a point of self-discovery at the journey's end. A change in living arrangements is frequently the first critical step in this direction.

CHANGE IN LIVING ARRANGEMENTS

Moving out of the marital home and back into the home of parents, into public or subsidized housing, into a shelter, or moving in and doubling up with relatives or friends is a major relocation decision. As the following case studies illustrate, initiating the first step can lead to new opportunities and a reduction in stress.

Moving Home

Moving back into the home of parents is a viable option when parents are supportive of the separation and willingly, not begrudgingly, open their home to a returning adult child and grandchild in need. Three benefits can accrue. First, housing costs may be substantially lower—or even free. Second, parents who are willing and able to provide child care services may do so at reduced cost, in return for services rendered by the single mother to help them. Third, when parents are supportive, they serve as an emotional buffer to both the returning mother and her children.

On the negative side, some living arrangements become overcrowded. In other instances, intergenerational living in close proximity can result in a "hovering" tendency in which parents appear intrusive to a single mother's efforts to start a new social life. If parents disapproved of their daughter's conduct during the marriage or subsequently, they may continue to express such feelings. A nonsupportive, negative living environment may emerge that strains the positive benefits associated with affordable housing and child care.

Mary Zagreb's situation illustrates how conflicts can and do develop, but when time and energy are invested in resolving those conflicts and reaching accommodations, a richer family life can result. Mary and her 4-year-old daughter moved back into her parents' two-family home when she separated from her abusive husband. She pays $700 a month rent and utilities, about 30 percent of the monthly income she earns as a hairdresser. The house is on a pleasant, tree-lined street in a city neighborhood. Mary is satisfied with her living arrangements because the apartment is spacious and clean; the area is safe yet near shopping and public transportation. Her mother takes care of the child at no cost while Mary works about 30 hours a week.

Mary had been divorced for a few years when she met a man with whom she fell in love. It was a wonderful relationship. They were very happy and planned to marry, when Mary got pregnant. When she told him she was pregnant, the man left, and she never saw him again. Her mother was furious at Mary. She encouraged her to have an abortion. Mary was worried that she would be thrown out of the house. She explains:

I had never felt truly alone until then. I was abandoned by the man I loved and then rejected by my own mother. Once I had the baby, she became supportive. She babysat for me so I could go right back to work. But our relationship had deep scars because of how angry she was at me during the second pregnancy and how angry I was at her for being so angry at me. . . . So she's both aggravating and vital. We have grown together over the past few years. She is now my best friend.

Family relationships weathered new turbulence wrought by the second pregnancy, and the ongoing turbulence of fear wrought by her abusive ex-husband, as described in Chapter 4.

Mary still lives in the same apartment in her parents' house. She is both grateful and regretful that she has to depend on them so much. This move back home in the Aftermath helped to transition her family into Realignment and ultimately to Stabilization. Mary and her two children have affordable housing, affordable child care, a safe neighborhood environment, housing near her employment, adequate income that includes earnings and child support, and a social support system. The road was not an easy one to travel for either Mary or her parents. But Mary considers herself and her children stable at last.

Moving Down

A move from an elegant, suburban three-bedroom home with a white picket fence into a rented two-bedroom trailer may be anathema for some, but for Edna Bernays it helped to stabilize her life and she does not regret it. She was brought up in an upper-middle-income family. During her marriage, her husband's $40,000 a year income continued to maintain a comfortable standard of living for her and her child. The marriage itself was a lonely and unhappy one from Edna's perspective, and she filed for divorce.

Her husband was allowed to keep the house in the property settlement because it had been in his family for years. There were no other assets to divide. The judge ordered her ex-husband to pay $400 a month in child support for the couple's 7-year-old child. Receipt of child support combined with her gross monthly income of $1,600 provided Edna with adequate total household income to afford a nice apartment in her small city, but she did not choose that option. Instead, she chose a low-cost trailer for three reasons: (1) the trailer was near her mother's home, (2) her mother provided free after-school child care, and (3) her employment situation was unstable and she might have to relocate at any time. She did not want to be tied down with a lease.

Edna is employed at a large shipyard on the Atlantic seaboard whose entire business is based on government contracts. Recent cutbacks in the Defense Department budget and downsizing and restructuring of military-related industries portend hundreds of layoffs at the shipyard in multiple job categories. With day-to-day worry about getting notice of termination, Edna did not want to be locked into a lease with high rent requirements, up-front cash for first and last months' rent, plus a security deposit.

The costs of her basic needs in the trailer are low—19 percent of her income for housing costs and free child care. This gives Edna the financial buffer she needs should she have to relocate again. If she is laid off, she is confident her mother would help her out financially and would let her move back into her parents' home.

Edna considers herself stable post-divorce. She realizes that by ending her marriage she gave up a lot. But to her, material possessions and appearances aren't everything. She says, "I am much happier living where I am as a lonely single parent than being desperately unhappy, lonely, and married living in a three-bedroom house with a white picket fence." The state of the economy is the largest force determining family stability now.

Moving Over, Doubling Up

Doubling up with another one-parent family or with relatives who also have children may seem overcrowded, but some single mothers find that it is a viable transition state. Maribelle Nance's circumstance illustrates how shared living arrangements can reduce work/family tensions for those who work "swing shifts" and also have opportunity to advance themselves through educational programs.

Maribelle and her husband had always rented their home during their marriage. Relocating to some form of rental housing was the only option available to Maribelle at separation. She worked nights as a pharmacy assistant in a hospital about thirty-two hours a week. Getting her own apartment was a consideration, but finding good, affordable evening and overnight child care for her two children, ages 10 and 8, was her biggest dilemma. Her total household income from earnings and $400 a month child support were insufficient to pay for a rental apartment and nighttime child care.

Maribelle's older sister and brother-in-law invited her and her children to live with them in a four-bedroom apartment they rented in a large, rambling two-family house. Her sister and brother-in-law had three children of their own. The new household was then composed of three adults and five children all under the age of 10.

Maribelle is satisfied with these living arrangements and very grateful to her sister and brother-in-law for their support. First, she pays only 21 percent of her household income to her sister and brother-in-law for room and board. Second, she can work the swing shift at the hospital at night knowing that trusted relatives are taking good care of her children. She, in turn, takes care of their children when they work during the day or want to go out. Third, a training opportunity developed at the hospital for work as an ultrasound technician, and Maribelle was able to sign up for it. Her sister and her brother-in-law are willing to help with the extra child care obligation at no extra cost. The program is offered through a local community college and will count toward college credits while advancing her employment opportunities at the same time.

Maribelle's living arrangements have lasted six months. She hopes to stay until she completes her ultrasound technician training program. She anticipates an upturned economy in this field that will offer excellent employment opportunities with good benefits. Perhaps then she can afford both an apartment and child care on her own wages.

Transitional Housing Programs

Transitional housing programs exist in some areas for targeted populations with multiple unmet needs. One type of transitional housing is for mothers with substance abuse problems—a long-neglected population of public health concern. Poor urban women are especially disadvantaged for four reasons:

1. They do not have health coverage to pay for private rehabilitation programs.

2. If they do go into a residential treatment program, they have no place for their children to go while they are away.

3. Even if they complete a recovery program, they go home to neighborhood poverty where association with addicted persons, frequently their male partner, is prevalent.

4. If their addiction becomes known to the state, the child protective services agency can take their children away from them if child abuse or neglect is determined.

Women who have been victims of domestic violence may turn to alcohol or drugs to dull the pain in their lives. Participation in a residential recovery program where mother and child can live as a family unit is a first step in recovery and moving on to a more stable state.

The inclusion of children in the living arrangement and provision for adequate child care are key elements that make such a program work for single mothers. It worked for Lucy Porter. Lucy had been in an abusive relationship with a man for ten years. Her partner earned his income selling drugs. Both of them were users. Lucy admits that she hit rock-bottom before she entered Women Together, a residential treatment program in the Roxbury section of Boston. Lucy was referred to the program by a social worker employed by the state Department of Social Services. As a recipient of public welfare, Lucy was eligible for limited state aid to cover the costs of residential treatment.

From the state's perspective, the policy rationale is that a timely investment in a single mother will result in potential recovery and family preservation, costing the state less in the long run for public welfare benefits, health-related expenses, potential jail time, and long-term foster care for the child. The budget allocation for this purpose is small, however. Limited public funding is allocated for substance abuse treatment in residential settings because such approaches are based on a "rehabilitation" model, and strong political sentiment exists for approaching substance abuse from a "punishment" model, or even incarceration.

Women Together is a small, nonprofit social service agency created specifically to address the residential treatment needs of addicted women with children. The agency's executive director comments that nearly all women treated at Women Together report a history of physical, sexual, or emotional/psychological abuse as children or in adult relationships. The agency prides itself on a recent finding that 80 percent of its former residents are now living substance-free lives.[4]

In 1985, the agency purchased an old three-story house in a residential section of the inner city, a mostly black neighborhood of other large, single-family and two-family houses. The property was renovated for the expressed purpose of serving both the housing and service needs of twelve women with children. Each bedroom accommodates a bed for the mother and a crib or bed for her child, and one bureau. There is a common kitchen where meals are collectively prepared and eaten. A separate room for child care is arranged with age-appropriate furnishings and toys. An office area is located to the right of the multilocked entry, and a living room with floor-to-ceiling bay windows is off to the left. All furnishings have been donated to the house, and bags of donated clothing sit in the hallway for residents.

Lucy stayed at Women Together for her full treatment plan. She participated in both individual and group therapy sessions run by professionally trained staff as well as by paraprofessionals, most of whom have "been there" as recovered substance abusers themselves. Lucy kept to the strict routine of house management and maintenance by following the rules and regulations regarding personal possessions, visitors, phone calls, and trips to outside appointments.

The state's investment paid off. Lucy recovered. She did not go back to the inner-city neighborhood she used to live in before entering the program. Instead, her sister, a widow with four children who lived in a suburb about 25 miles outside the city, let her double-up with her. This living arrangement enabled Lucy to *realign* for several months, a time in which she applied for public and subsidized housing in the vicinity of her sister's home.

Nine months later, Lucy was selected for tenancy in a new housing complex. It is a fifty-unit rental development in which the real estate developer got tax benefits and a below-market interest loan to set aside ten units for low-income families. Lucy and her daughter are one of those ten families living in what is commonly called mixed-income housing. The property is well maintained, safe, and affordable. Her daughter is enrolled in the community's well-regarded school system.

At 34, Lucy is now employed, drug-free, and stable at last. She stresses that it was *very hard* ; the hardest part, she says, "is learning to stand alone and be okay without expecting a man to take care of you."

NEW STRUCTURES, ROLES, AND RESPONSIBILITIES

Transition from a two-parent to a single-parent form requires adjustment to the composition of the new family and to "the invisible set of functional demands that organizes the ways in which family members interact."[5] The key issue is how a mother successfully parents alone. Parental power is often conveyed by how a parent exercises control. In one-parent families, that pattern is usually changed. "Wait 'til your father gets home" no longer fits. Everyone must make adjustments.

The central question becomes: Who is in charge? The parent, as executive of the family unit, is charged with the parenting functions, defined as "a process of providing love and encouragement, the opportunities for experience and growth, the atmosphere of care and concern . . . a process for 'making children mind,' keeping them from 'growing up too fast,' and keeping them 'on the right track.' " [6]

While the parent does not have to do all these things alone, the ideal is that the parent ensures that these processes are carried out on behalf of children. In real life, family roles vary a great deal, but four structures form the basis of most arrangements: sole executive parent, auxiliary parent, unrelated substitute, and related substitute.

The Sole Executive Parent

The sole executive parent is the only adult involved in the basic care of the children in the home. She may consider herself the only person available to meet all family needs and perform all household chores. She runs the risk of overload on all levels—physically, psychologically, and socially. She tries to do the impossible, be both mother and father in an effort to make up for the father's absence. This supermom is bound to fail if she applies a two-parent role model to the new family form.

At the other end of the scale is the sole executive who perceives herself as a contributing coordinator rather than a direct supplier of all goods, services, and emotions to her children. She requires even young children to set the table, pick up toys, help with food preparation, and clean up. This approach builds on internal family resources thast serve to strengthen the family unit.[7]

A "time out" period for sole executive parents is useful. It creates a buffer zone to transition from the stress of work to the stress of evening meals, household chores, and parenting. Some mothers request ten minutes, and others thirty minutes. They go to their bedrooms and lie down to rest long enough to re-group for the next set of responsibilities. Children, of course, must respect the request.

In a study of male-headed and female-headed families in Mexican shanty towns, Sylvia Chant (1985) found that formation of a female-headed family resulted in family life becoming more secure and stable in many ways.

Sexual discrimination in the labor market often meant that women earned low wages, but these earnings were boosted by the economic cooperation of her children. Difficulties in carrying out the two full-time roles of homemaker and wage earner were smoothed out by the help of both male and female children in the home. Furthermore, an absence of violence within the family resulted in greater psychological security.[8]

The Auxiliary Parent

The auxiliary parent is usually the father of one or more of the children. He does not live with the family but shares one or more of the parental responsibilities with the single mother. Fathers who do not have custody usually have visitation rights and can be potent forces in the lives of their children. Physical absence from the home should not be taken as evidence that fathers have little interest in or contact with the family.[9]

Clarity about rules and manner of participation is critical in cases of joint custody. This arrangement requires both parents to share equally the responsibility for the physical, moral, and emotional development of their children; to share both rights and responsibilities for making decisions that affect their children; and to share joint physical custody by having the child live with each parent for a substantial period of time. In many instances, the child moves back and forth between each parent's home or apartment. In other instances, the parents move in and out of the same house on a planned schedule to accommodate joint custody. Joint custody means that a child may actually be part of two single-parent families, or one single-parent family and one step-parent family. Rules and patterns of behavior will obviously be different on some level in the two households. Charlene Fabiani's case presented in Chapter 7 outlined the difficulties and stresses of attaining family stability with this model when one parent has stable living arrangements and the other does not.

Joint custody presents distinctive parental challenges. Some argue that joint custody represents an "increasingly frantic legal effort to maintain the illusion of the nuclear family, even when it no longer exists," that the term "joint custody is often applied to a legislated pseudonuclearity."[10] Specific help may be essential to facilitate the renegotiation of family structures in these cases. The two households may be strikingly different since the two parents are no longer living as husband and wife and therefore would have no need to work on shaping a unified family culture. Sonia Sager's experience, presented in Chapter 5, is a case example of this conflict.

The Unrelated or Related Substitute

The unrelated substitute is a person who is not related to the family but shares one or more parental functions. The related substitute is a relative who assumes a role of parent to the children. In both of these arrangements, either related or unrelated persons assume some responsibility for parental functions, sometimes for long periods of time. Two single mothers and their children who double-up in the same house exemplify the unrelated substitute structure in that they are assuming a financial function that reduces the overall financial burden. A mother who cohabits with a man who assumes the emotional and financial responsibilities of a father's role is also an unrelated substitute.

Grandparents have historically stepped in as related substitute parents. A trend toward grandparents as sole related substitute developed when neither a child's father nor mother was able to care for the child alone. The role of substance abuse in family disintegration caused some fathers and mothers to enter long-term residential treatment centers without their children. Some went to jail. Others just disappeared. The courts gave custody of the children to grandparents when possible and appropriate. A national organization emerged to serve as a network and support system for men and women in their 40s, 50s, and 60s who find themselves raising small grandchildren at a time many expected to have an empty nest and plan for retirement.

PERSONAL ADJUSTMENT

Supportive families and/or participation in mutual aid groups are key to helping single mothers reach a point of personal autonomy and independence. Such personal adjustment gives power and control over one's life—a happy ending to the years spent in the turbulent phases of the *Aftermath* and *Realignment*. Those without supportive families or groups of friends or acquaintances often do not make it to *Stabilization*; they remain socially isolated and economically marginalized.

Role of Family

The role of a supportive family is key in helping a one-parent family stabilize itself, as illustrated by the foregoing cases. "I couldn't have done it without them," is a common theme expressed by single mothers regardless of age or marital status. A single parent without family support is greatly disadvantaged in housing options, in offers of financial assistance, in donated benefits such as car sharing or free child care, and in emotional and social supports to buffer the stresses of doing it all alone. Close friends also form supportive networks that become a "family of choice" for those without blood relatives willing or able to offer the necessary help.

Role of Mutual Aid Groups

Participation in informal support or mutual aid groups formed expressly to give voice to the needs of parents alone is a major source of assistance with personal adjustment to single mothers. Three types of groups stand out. One type is set within the confines of nonprofit social service agencies that run therapeutic groups. A second are religious-based groups that seek to support the basic needs of separated, divorced, or never-married parents. These groups provide valuable spiritual anchors that strengthen individuals through group counseling, and informal networks that offer social and economic support whenever needed. The third type are wide-reaching social groups composed of men and women ready to connect again in social relationships through group recreational activities, parties, dances, and special events.

Community-based social service agencies offer group sessions to help single parents cope with the strains of their parenting roles. Such agencies see children and adults for individual or family counseling. Group counseling is a therapeutic intervention that can focus on a range of issues including parenting frail elders, substance abuse, eating disorders, and bereavement. Once the group is formed and the process begins, it is considered a "closed" group and no new members are added. The group process unfolds over a prescribed number of sessions—six, nine, or twelve weeks duration. Attendance is required at all group meetings.

The Arbor Youth Counseling Clinic offers one example of the role that mutual aid groups can play in helping mothers cope with multiple issues. When the clinic began their group, they did not expect such long-term benefits. The group began when one social worker realized that five women she counseled on an individual basis had a lot in common. They were all single mothers in psychological distress because they were isolated and had no family supports. They were all struggling to raise children alone while juggling jobs and child care. She decided to introduce them to each other and see if they would like to form a group.

The women, ranging in age from 32 to 43, were diverse in other ways. One was never-married, the others were separated or divorced; two lived in public housing, one was a renter, and two were homeowners. Two were on public welfare, one was a lawyer, and two were in clerical positions.

The group was supposed to meet weekly for a prescribed number of sessions and then terminate. The bonds among the women had become so strong, however, that they would not stop meeting. The commitment to the group was inviolate. The women needed to keep the support network intact.

The agency allowed the group to meet there once a week. The same group of five women has done just that—for the past *ten years*. Members believe the group has enriched their individual and collective lives in five ways over the past decade:

1. They have shared information and solved problems together on tough child discipline issues, particularly drugs and alcohol, and the unexpected dilemmas posed by raising boys alone.
2. They have supported and encouraged each other to go back to court on child support enforcement and modification of child support orders.
3. They have shared information and passed on referrals for good child care providers and for job opportunities.
4. They have encouraged each other to go back to school for more education and training.
5. They have developed respect for and appreciation of each other's differences.

In one sense, the members became a surrogate cheerleading squad for one another. They emphasize that one important lesson was learned as a result of their experience: gender, family structure, and role responsibilities are more binding factors than class, place of residence, and source and amount of income. They learned that, in the final analysis, they were really all the same.

None of the women has remarried, although they say they are still hopeful, if they could find the right relationship.

Self-Discovery

Those who traveled the long and bumpy road from Aftermath to Stabilization suggest that lessons are learned at journey's end:

- Reflect on your goals and dreams, but learn to make compromises and accommodations along the way.
- Do not victimize yourself. Autonomy and independence offer control and power over one's own life.

- Reach out to others for help and seek as many sources of support as possible.
- Use the trip as an opportunity to find out who you really are. Discover personal strengths as well as weaknesses. Confidence will build. You will find your own "voice." Then learn to speak with it.
- Have adventures. Take care of yourself.

SUMMARY

There are three stages of development through which a family will pass on the way to stability following marital dissolution: the Aftermath, Realignment, and Stabilization. The Aftermath stage is a longer and more difficult stage to navigate in the 1990s than is commonly appreciated. The level of environmental complexity impedes family realignment because of the instability of housing arrangements and fluctuations in the levels and sources of income. Families can be in a prolonged state of crisis for years, postponing attention to restructuring new roles and responsibilities within the family.

Nonetheless, individual actions can expedite the transition toward a more stable state by (1) making changes in living arrangements, (2) developing new family structures, roles, and responsibilities, and (3) seeking help with personal adjustment from supportive sources. The Realignment stage may require several adjustments forward in its rebuilding phase all leading forward to stabilization.

Being a head-of-household and living alone with children is not necessarily synonymous with being stable. Doubling up with family or friends in a living arrangement that all consider satisfactory and affordable, where support and assistance are given and received, may be the stable state for certain families. Affordable, stable housing, reliable income, and a personal support system ultimately facilitate family stabilization.

NOTES

1. See, for example, Fredda Herz Brown, "The Post Divorce Family" and Monica McGoldrick "Women and the Family Life Cycle" in Monica McGoldrick and Betty Carter, eds., *The Changing Family Life Cycle* (Boston: Allyn and Bacon, 1989).

2. Ibid.

3. Ibid.

4. Personal Interview with Ellerwee Gadson, Executive Director, Women, Inc., Boston, May 1993.

5. Salvador Minuchin, *Families and Family Therapy* (Cambridge, Mass.: Harvard University Press, 1974).

6. Gary Crow, *The Nurturing Family* (Milbrae, Calif.: Celestial Arts, 1980).

7. Helen A. Mendez, "Single-Parent Families: A Topology of Life Styles," *Social Work* 24 (May 1979): 193–200.

8. Sylvia Chant, "Single-Parent Families: Choice or Constraint: The Formation of Female-headed Households in Mexican Shanty Towns," *Development and Change* 16 (1985): 649.

9. Mendez, "Single-Parent Families," pp. 193–200.

10. Richard N. Atkins, "Single Mothers and Joint Custody: Common Ground," in *In Support of Families*, eds. Michael W. Yogman and T. Berry Brazelton (Cambridge, Mass.: Harvard University Press, 1986).

—9—

Family Futures in a Caring Society

A caring society is one where people need not lose their dignity if they are ill or fall on hard times or simply grow old; where each child is encouraged to fulfill his or her talents; and where people can live like human beings. The humane city is the built form of the caring society.

John R. Short[1]

This book has tried to explain why single mothers are uprooted, are on the edge of society, and how and why they linger there. We have seen that single mothers have diverse family characteristics but similar life experiences. Their gender and role responsibilities as *female sole* family breadwinners and *sole* caregivers suggest complex workplace requirements, few housing choices, and conflicting societal expectations.

A single mother faces an uphill battle because her basic needs for housing, stability, economic security, and personal safety and security are intricately linked together, while private-sector and community, state, and federal policy responses to these needs are fragmented and uncertain. For example, when a woman earns low wages, she cannot afford to maintain her home. If the family moves frequently in search of more affordable rent, she is unable to maintain a stable job. If she works long hours demanded by her job, her ex-husband, neighbors, or the state may file charges for neglecting her children. If she is very poor, she and her children may end up homeless. If her survival strategy to domestic violence is to leave her home, she and her children may end up without income or housing. If she resorts to public welfare as her only source of income, she will receive a monthly allotment that is insufficient to pay for shelter in most urban areas.

In the United States, family policy does not link labor market, housing, or income maintenance policies in any coherent manner that might function in concert toward one goal—family stability. As demonstrated in Chapters 4, 5, 6, and 7, it is noteworthy that single mothers and their families stabilize at all in social and physical environments hostile to them. Single mothers of color, whose voices are heard in preceding chapters, illustrate how resilience and fortitude helped them survive the living conditions in concentrated urban poverty.

Single-parent families *could* establish a secure family foundation if

- Policymakers and the public at large had an informed understanding of who single parents are, why they make the choices they make, and the consequences of these choices.
- Policies for employment, housing, income maintenance, domestic violence, and child support were linked.
- The *vision* of a caring society guided the allocation of America's resources to provide livable and humane cities where children and families matter.

This concluding chapter addresses each of these points. It is argued that urban policy *is* family policy. Attempts to respond to single-parent family needs must consider the cross-cutting nature of decisions made in the public domain on quality of life and life choices of single-parent families (indeed of all families) in the private domain. Specific recommendations are set forth.

NATIONAL URBAN POLICY IS FAMILY POLICY

Cities are reeling from the impacts of two decades of economic, social, and political change: corporate restructuring, absorption of new waves of immigration, a changing market in illegal drugs, gang violence, racial tension, political disinterest, and disinvestment. A priority of the mid-1990s should be to restructure America's urban centers into livable cities with an engaged workforce, community involvement in economic activity, and a better quality of family and working life. Key policy areas will be economic development, housing and neighborhood development, drug interdiction, public health (i.e., substance abuse treatment, reduction in infant mortality, family planning counseling, confrontation of crime, illegal drugs, and violence), income maintenance, education, and human services—topics that are not usually tied together under the umbrella of *Family Policy*, and yet are critical influences on the lives of urban families. Connecting these substantive areas in a meaningful way will require greater coordination among intergovernmental agencies at the federal, state, and local levels; admittedly, this is a difficult task, but it is a necessary one.

Typically, Family Policy is confined to dimensions of poverty, and thus to income maintenance policies for public welfare and child support. These are very important areas of social and economic concern that are more fully addressed by others.[2] This chapter focuses on recommendations intended to blunt the impacts of existing urban policies on low-wage, single mothers. The cross-cutting effects of housing and employment, of domestic violence and housing, of public welfare and work, of child support and housing are documented in the preceding chapters. Therefore, there is a clear public interest in the interactive affects of these policies.

The following recommendations represent a starting point in thinking about restructuring cities into livable, humane places for families and children: bridging urban-suburban linkages; reducing concentrated urban poverty; fighting drugs, crime, and violence; promoting community actions for affordable housing and services; restructuring urban education for 1990s job skills; and combining sources of family economic support.

Urban-Suburban Linkages

Bridges must be built with suburban communities. Cities are the engine of the national economy and the cultural and intellectual centers. Declining cities lead to declining suburbs. As aggressive as suburbs are in separating themselves from urban problems, recent studies reveal that suburbs cannot quarantine themselves from a troubled economy, widening disparities in income, and rising poverty.[3] Suburbanites need to understand their stake in urban development. Money spent on urban revitalization will also improve suburban living.

Reducing Concentrated Urban Poverty

Cities would be more livable if existing concentrations of poverty were dispersed. We must reduce the isolation of poor families through public and private partnerships in economic development, regional job mobility, and dispersed affordable housing.

Public and Private Partnerships in Economic Development. Real estate developers can revitalize rundown, abandoned sections of cities, make the areas habitable for families, and turn a profit by including a range of housing options for different income groups as a central element in the plan. Such large-scale projects require both commercial and residential development—shopping centers to meet consumer needs, buildings that contain neighborhood services, and housing.

One example of this approach is Westminster Place in the west-central corridor of St. Louis, Missouri. The project goal was to physically, economically, and socially revitalize a rundown, 90-acre parcel of inner-city land. Public subsidies from federal and local programs were used as incentives for the private developer to include a wide range of housing opportunities within the project: rehabilitation of existing buildings that appealed to long-time neighborhood residents; new construction of garden apartment complexes for those who can pay the market or going rent, those who have moderate, partially subsidized units, and very low-income who require larger subsidies.

The "mixed-income" housing approach was an interesting aspect of the project. Low- and moderate-income residents live side by side as neighbors in the *same* apartment complex, further integrating households by income as well as by race. Attractive physical design, strict tenant selection criteria, and attentive property management practices have made this project a stable residential community while economically revitalizing the entire area.[4] While mixed-income housing has been developed to both implement federal social purpose and meet local needs, for the last 30 years it has received little research attention as a building block for economic development.

Regional Job Mobility. Another approach is to monitor job creation with a focus on regional employment. Clean air, clean water, and good roads are understood to be public goods that require regional and state planning as well as common provision. The emergence of job opportunities in the suburbs and in newly developed urban centers far removed from workers in older central cities requires regional planning for job mobility. Three areas should be considered: (1) inner-city worker training for suburban jobs, (2) information about and referral to these new sources of employment, and (3) a restructuring of public transportation systems to facilitate outbound journeys.[5]

Tenant-Based Housing Subsidies. A dispersal strategy of tenant-based subsidies throughout a metropolitan region could deconcentrate those families who seek suburban or urban racially and economically diverse communities. Housing search services and a metropolitan focus that link individual tenant to individual landlord—as in the Gautreaux Program—will be required.

Fighting Drugs and Violence

The role of substance abuse in domestic violence, family disintegration, and crime is a critical, strategic issue. The complexity of the role illegal drugs play in society defies traditional solutions. Fundamental changes in the market of illegal drugs have increased street violence, gang involvement, and wide-open drug dealing that was not present in American cities a generation ago. The emergence of crack in the 1980s made low-risk, exorbitant-profit trafficking tempting to many, including, but not limited to, organized crime, urban gangs, and corrupt law enforcement officers. Some cities now spend more on jails than on public education.[6] The impotence of costly local methods to cope with what is really an international drug problem is a central question in any policy debate about cities and families.

Community Actions for Affordable Housing and Services

Local planning boards have extensive power to help stabilize families with children through approval of permits for a variety of housing types and community services appropriate to meeting the needs of 1990s families. Accessory apartments in single-family homes, multifamily housing, home-based occupations, group homes, or child care centers are frequently not allowed by local zoning ordinances that were created for a different era.

Zoning ordinances regulate the use of land. The need for zoning emerged to guide development of massive new housing subdivisions that sprang up across the country after World War II. Demographic changes, however, indicate that family form has changed dramatically. Housing needs are different, but housing and community development responses have not kept pace. Residential displacement can be avoided if communities approach public decisions with the goal of preserving and stabilizing families. In particular, archaic zoning restrictions must be eased to permit the development of more appropriate housing, accessory apartments, group homes and services, and child care opportunities.

Changing Development Standards for Housing. Zoning and subdivision regulations that guided the development of tract housing in the 1960s and 1970s are inappropriate for townhouses, duplexes, cluster developments, mobile homes, and apartment complexes that dominate today's housing market. Local communities need to update their development standards to fit the changing needs of the housing market and make housing more affordable.

Accessory Apartments. Accessory apartments are small apartments carved out of unused spaces in larger one-family homes. Most communities have zoning ordinances that prohibit the creation of such apartments so that the character, value, and quality of neighborhoods composed of single-family homes can be protected. With appropriate community interest, accessory apartments can be properly regulated and, at the same time, bring many benefits to certain community residents while being ideal housing opportunities for single parents:

- The economic benefit of additional rental income allows elderly homeowners to stay in their own homes, undisplaced from stable and secure living arrangements. Older persons whose own families are now grown find themselves alone and "overhoused" in large family homesteads with too much space to heat and too many maintenance chores to perform. The mortgage may be paid, making the monthly costs affordable, but the costs of painting, repairs, yard work, and other necessary maintenance may be too high. Rental income from otherwise unused space helps to defray these maintenance costs that improve the property and contribute to neighborhood quality.

- The location of accessory apartments in many larger homes offers safe neighborhood environments in areas with good schools, which single-parent families seek.

- Social benefits accrue to an elderly homeowner and a single-mother tenant who reduce the social isolation each might experience living independently. For example, a tenant could assist an elderly owner with shopping or chores. In return, the owner might befriend the child and mother, bringing friendship, intergenerational maturity, and emotional support into their lives. For both, the isolation and loneliness of independent living give way to social supports and connections.

- Single mothers who are homeowners reap the same economic and social benefits. The added income allows them to stay put and avoid housing displacement.

- This approach does not rely on public funds or private developers for the provision of affordable housing. It is a community-based model negotiated between owner and renter.

Housing and Social Services. Group homes provide services for specific populations of people with common needs. However, zoning too frequently stymies the development of such shared living arrangements. Three types of group homes provide much needed support to single mothers:

- Battered women's shelters are needed that provide temporary shelter, food, and social services to mothers and children so they can leave abusive relationships.

- Transitional housing is a next step for women who need support services and group living to learn the basic skills required for independent living. This option is especially worthwhile for adolescent mothers who are trying to finish high school or GED programs, enter job-training programs, begin employment, juggle child care routines, and parent infants and small children at the same time. Most have never lived on their own before. Viewed as an educational, service-intensive housing situation, transitional housing is a key stepping stone to independence.

- Residential treatment programs are needed for those mothers with children who want to end their reliance on drugs and alcohol. Such group homes are also service-intensive and require strict adherence to house rules and regulations.

Child Care Everywhere. There is a critical shortage of quality child care for working mothers near where they live or work. A lack of affordable, accessible child care is a destabilizing force for single-mother families. Although employers should include on-site child care centers as an incentive to attract and keep good workers, communities also must accept responsibility for caring for their young.

Child care operations are prohibited by zoning ordinances in certain residential neighborhoods. Neighborhood residential needs must be balanced with the community's need for child care that meet requirements of federal and state law. Innovative local programs that increase and improve child care options are essential.

Home Occupation. Working at home is a growing phenomenon among men and women in the information age of telecommunications. Many women, however, have not yet attained skills for this computer-based work but have other home-based work they can perform such as child care, crafts, catering, typing, and hairdressing. Zoning has traditionally prohibited home-based occupations in certain residential neighborhoods for fear of disturbing neighbors with noise or traffic. Home-based occupations offer single mothers an ideal situation to balance their breadwinner/caregiver roles. Adequate community attention is needed to stimulate home-based occupations while not detracting from the residential quality of the neighborhood.

Restructuring Urban Education for 1990s Jobs

A major restructuring of urban education and training is needed to better prepare urban youth for high-skilled employment requirements of 1990s jobs. Urban school systems must reexamine their mission to educate and train both teenage boys and girls to (1) value education as the only viable avenue to achieve employment security and (2) provide a relevant curriculum that provides an adequate knowledge base and technical competence.

A new conceptualization is needed for the education of girls. First, girls must appreciate the reality that labor force participation will be required of them throughout their adult lives whether or not they have children. A responsive educational preparation must stress knowledge, skills, and values that prepare boys as well as girls to accept girls as equal citizens in the educational process.

Urban education faces formidable challenges: poverty of family resources; violent neighborhood environments from which students come; destabilizing influence of youths who are in and out of the revolving door to school, to courtrooms, to jail, and to school; gang cultures; multilinguistic populations; teenage parents; and the pervasive and domineering counterculture of drugs. Public instruction is needed in nontraditional locations in order to reach the educational goals of a diverse student population: in public housing developments, in social service agencies, in prisons, and in homeless shelters.

Public/private partnerships are needed wherein the private sector assumes responsibility and leadership for the direction of the public educational enterprise. Private corporations should "lend" their executives to public schools in urban areas to volunteer as teachers and administrators as they do in providing technical assistance to nonprofit agencies through the United Way and other endeavors. This hands-on experience would offer corporate decision makers a realistic view from the streets to help forge educational solutions to the current mismatch between needed labor market skills, environmental stressors confronting urban youth, and political decisions made by entrenched school boards.

Finally, public investment in education must increase because quality education can *prevent* economic insecurity. Some states currently spend five times more to incarcerate a criminal than to educate a child.[7] Economic security has more chance to develop when states decide to spend five times more to educate children in the front end than to incarcerate offenders in the back end.

COMBINING SOURCES OF ECONOMIC SUPPORT

The economic conditions of the 1990s require family economic and social support from every possible source: family members, local communities, state and federal governments, private agencies, and employer-based work/family benefits. *Both* parents—not just mothers—must be held accountable and assume responsibility for the economic support of their own children. Societal expectations of absent fathers are very low. This is observed in the parental work requirements of the Welfare Reform Act of 1988 and in years of congressional foot-dragging in the passage of federal child support legislation.[8]

Welfare-to-Work and Income Packaging

Ending dependency on public assistance will require far more than transitioning welfare mothers into low-wage work. Independence will require a fundamental policy shift that allows for "income packaging" of multiple economic sources: wages with public welfare benefits, child support, health insurance, and subsidized housing. Independence will come when the family is stable.

Although one relatively small element in the Welfare Reform Act of 1988 trains and educates fathers who are unemployed and unable to pay child support, the policy goal of the legislation puts responsibility for family economic support squarely on the mother's shoulders. Once again, she receives no relief from the role burden, while absent fathers are kept at the periphery of parental financial obligation.

Existing incremental welfare changes merely penalize the mother for trying to work her way out of poverty. For example, employed low-wage single parents teeter on the brink of public welfare dependency. A woman or man working at minimum wage ($4.50/hour), full-time, full-year, has gross earnings of $9,360 annually, regardless of family size. In 1990, any three-person family with income below $10,419 and any four-person family with income below $13,359 was considered poor by the U.S. government. No state pays enough in public welfare to keep a family above these levels. The average AFDC benefit is the United States is $4,400 a year, plus food stamps and Medicaid health benefits.

Today, if a woman tries to work her way off of welfare, her benefits are reduced dollar for dollar with earnings. Public administrators and experts argue that unless a woman works full-time, is paid at least 50 percent above the prevailing minimum wage, receives full medical benefits, and has low child care costs she will be back on public welfare.[9] Despite the intent of the Welfare Reform Act of 1988 to end dependency, the structure of the market economy, limited public resource allocations for affordable housing, child care services, and regulations of the public welfare system itself do not make work pay for low-wage single parents.

Child Support

Child support enforcement and administrative reforms must take the burden of collecting child support off the shoulders of single mothers. The current system of child support is a maze of complexity and confusion. For example, action is required by federal, state, and local governments. Intervention is also required by the administrative, legislative, and judicial branches of government. The backlogged judiciary hears each case on an individual basis.

Absent parents who do not pay but are capable of paying adequate child support benefit from the system's inefficiencies. Custodial parents who seek to collect, modify, or increase child support orders abhor the excessive time demands and the pervasive gender bias evidenced in court orders.[10]

New child support legislation requires employers to deduct child support from the absent parent's paycheck and forward it to the state or the custodial parent as indicated. This method does not secure support for those children whose fathers are unemployed or underemployed and unable to pay child support at all. The following approaches are suggested to balance family support roles more equitably:

- Absent fathers who are not paying child support and are unemployed or underemployed should be mandated to enroll in education and skills training, job search, job placement, and job maintenance.
- Those who cannot locate or sustain jobs to help support their children should be required to work full-time, full-year, in targeted projects whose goal is to upgrade and improve housing and community environments. Some examples include rehabilitating public housing projects, turning abandoned buildings into habitable family rental housing, and refurbishing public school buildings and grounds.

Pay Equity

When all is said and done, an overriding issue in developing economic security for one-parent families, regardless of whether they live in the city, the suburbs, or rural areas, is the complex problem of the wage gap—the pay differentials between what women and men earn. Compounding the gender pay gap is the huge growth during the 1980s in the wage gap between those, regardless of gender, with a college education and those without, between those with nonmanual jobs and those with manual jobs, between those with experience and those without.[11]

While the gender pay gap closed from 58 cents on the dollar in 1971 to 69 cents on the dollar in 1988, the increase in overall wage inequality threatens both future gains and those already made. Although women have increased their labor market skills, they are swimming upstream in a market that has become increasingly unfavorable to people with lower labor market experience. Many factors contribute to the wage gap, particularly different patterns of labor force affiliation between men and women during the early child-rearing years, women's skills, and the nature of the jobs most women perform.

Women's education and skills and their treatment in the workplace must improve before a positive change in the wage gap will be seen.[12] Yet in the 1980s a backlash to women's advancement virtually halted what had been a vigorous drive for women's equality in the workplace in the 1960s and 1970s.[13] The Supreme Court called into question the legality of specific aspects of affirmative action and also limited the ability of persons to seek remedies to alleged biases in the workplace. The Equal Employment Opportunity Commission (EEOC) reduced its active litigation against corporations that excluded women from entire occupational categories.

The Civil Rights Act of 1991 marked a shift in the trends of the 1980s. The antidiscrimination provisions of the legislation applied to employers in both the public and private sectors and reaffirmed the ability of employees to bring "disparate impact lawsuits" (lawsuits alleging that specific hiring or promotion decisions adversely affected women, racial minorities, or other minorities) under Title VII of the Civil Rights Act of 1964. The legislation also allowed workers to seek monetary damages in cases of alleged intentional discrimination.[14]

Thus, an economically secure family future for single mothers rests on multiple, and often complex, work/family issues that affect all women, especially those with children. To achieve economic equality for women ultimately requires societal acceptance that financial independence for women through waged work is beneficial for families and for the wider society. The life choices of single mothers will improve dramatically when the gender pay gap closes and when a single mother's high costs of working are reduced.

SUMMARY

A stable future for one-parent families hinges on four factors: (1) societal values that respect all family forms, (2) gender equality for women in the home, in the workplace, and in public institutions, (3) affordable, permanent housing, and (4) workplace opportunity to earn a family wage.

The influence of economic growth on women's employment prospects is central to family stability. Until women's and men's educational attainment and job skills match the increased demand for well-educated workers, we can expect current trends to continue: there will be fewer marriages; more young adults will postpone marriages; more births will occur outside of marriage; there will be more diverse living arrangements in families and households; the number of one-parent families will increase.

While policy-making still takes place in an adversarial arena, family issues are beginning to be taken seriously. The federal policy-making process is a conservative one, and only incremental change can be expected. However, it is in the interest of both the public and private sectors to pay attention to the full range of family policies as defined here, especially as they impact the basic needs of single-mother, low-wage workers in particular.

Not investing in such families sets them up to fail. A self-fulfilling prophecy relegates poor families to social and economic isolation when, with coordinated income and housing "packages" to support their own motivation and personal work efforts, they could become stable families and productive workers. The development of responsive policies by local, state, and federal governments and by private-sector employers is an important and necessary step to increase economic, housing, and personal security.

In the long term, the future of one-parent families—and the life-chances of the children raised in them—will depend on a commitment to a caring society. Only then will societal norms mandate humane cities in which family stability is possible where all family members have the opportunity to develop self-worth and human dignity in violence-free living environments.

NOTES

1. For an in-depth discussion of humane cities in a caring society, see John R. Short, *The Humane City* (Oxford, England: Basil Blackwell Ltd., 1989).

2. Mary Jo Bane and David Ellwood, *Single Mothers and Their Living Arrangements*, Report prepared for the Department of Health and Human Services (Cambridge, Mass.: Harvard University, 1984), mimeo; Sheila B. Kamerman and Alfred J. Kahn, "What Europe Does for Single-Parent Families," *The Public Interest*, 1989, pp. 70–86; Sheila B. Kamerman and Alfred Kahn, *Mothers Alone: Strategies for a Time of Change* (Dover, Mass.: Auburn House Publishing Co.,

1988); M. Maclean and L. Weitzman, eds., *Economic Consequences of Divorce: The International Perspective* (Oxford, England: Clarendon Press, 1992); David T. Ellwood, *Poor Support: Poverty in the American Family* (New York: Basic Books, 1988); and Mimi Abramovitz, *Regulating the Lives of Women* (Boston: South End Press, 1988).

3. Peter Dreier, "Bush to Cities: Drop Dead," *The Progressive* 56, No. 7 (July 1992): 22.

4. For a more in-depth analysis of this model, see Mulroy, "Mixed-Income Housing in Action," *Urban Land* 50, No. 5 (May 1991): 2–7. 1991.

5. M. Hughes, "Employment Decentralization and Accessibility: A Strategy for Stimulating Regional Mobility," *Journal of the American Planning Association* 57, No. 3 (Summer 1991): 288–298.

6. *Newsweek*, October 11, 1993, p. 34; Sean Flynn, "How Safe Is Your Town?" *Boston Magazine*, September 1993, pp. 114, 116–117.

7. See, for example, Massachusetts Department of Corrections and Massachusetts Department of Education, Office of Research, as reported to Massachusetts Budget Office, fiscal year 1993.

8. See, for example, Anne L. Radigan, "Federal Policy-making and Family Issues," in *Women As Single Parents: Confronting Institutional Barriers in the Courts, the Workplace, and the Housing Markets*, ed. Elizabeth A. Mulroy (Dover, Mass.: Auburn House Publishing Co., 1988).

9. David Ellwood, "The Changing Structure of American Families," *Journal of the American Planning Association* 59, No. 1 (Winter 1993): 3–8.

10. Lynn Hecht Schafran, "Gender Bias in the Courts," in *Women As Single Parents: Confronting Institutional Barriers in the Courts, the Workplace, and the Housing Markets*, ed. Elizabeth A. Mulroy (Dover, Mass.: Auburn House Publishing Co., 1988).

11. *Harvard Business Review* 71, No. 5, September/October 1993: 10–11.

12. Ibid., p. 11.

13. For an in-depth examination of this point, see Susan Faludi, *Backlash: The Undeclared War Against American Women* (New York: Crown Publishing Co., 1991).

14. Bruce Janssen, *The Reluctant Welfare State*, 2nd ed. (Pacific Grove, Calif.: Brooks/Cole Publishing Co., 1993).

Bibliography

Abrahamse, Allan, Peter Morrison, and Linda Waite. "Beyond Stereotypes: Who Becomes a Single Teenage Mother?" Research Report, The RAND Publication Series. Santa Monica, Calif.: The RAND Corporation, 1988.

Abramovitz, Mimi, and Fred Newdom. "Talking Back to the Welfare Bashers," *Bertha Capen Reynolds Society Newsletter*. 4, No. 3 (Spring 1992).

Abramovitz, Mimi. *Regulating the Lives of Women*. Boston: South End Press, 1988.

Ahlburg, Dennis A., and Carol J. DeVita. "New Realities of the American Family," *Population Bulletin* 47, No. 2 (Washington, D.C.: Population Reference Bureau, August 1992): 1–44.

American Medical Association. "Domestic Violence: No Longer a Family Secret." In *Five Issues in American Health*. Chicago, 1991.

Amott, Teresa. "Working for Less: Single Mothers in the Workplace." In *Women As Single Parents: Confronting Institutional Barriers in the Courts, the Workplace, and the Housing Market*, ed. Elizabeth A. Mulroy. Dover, Mass.: Auburn House Publishing Co., 1988.

Atkins, Richard N. "Single Mothers and Joint Custody: Common Ground." In *In Support of Families*, eds. Michael W. Yogman and T. Berry Brazelton. Cambridge, Mass.: Harvard University Press, 1986.

Bane, Mary Jo, and David Ellwood. *Single Mothers and Their Living Arrangements*. Report prepared for the Department of Health and Human Services. Cambridge, Mass.: Harvard University, 1984, mimeo.

Bartlett, Susan. "Residential Mobility and Housing Choices for Single-Parent Mothers." Unpublished paper prepared for the Department of Housing and Urban Development by the Joint Center for Urban Studies of M.I.T. and Harvard University, Cambridge, Mass., 1980.

Beauvoir, S. de. *The Second Sex*, ed. H. M. Parshley. New York: Knopf, 1953.

Belle, D. "Poverty and Women's Mental Health." *American Psychologist* 45 (1990): 385–389.

Benning, Victoria. "Head of Boston School Panel Seeks Law Linking Parents to Children's Crimes." *The Boston Globe*, November 13, 1993, pp. 1 and 9.

Berry, Brian J. L. "The Counterurbanization Process: Urban America Since 1970." In *Urbanization and Counterurbanization*, ed. Brian J. L. Berry. *Urban Affairs Annual Reviews 11*. Beverly Hills, Calif.: Sage Publications, 1976.

Blakely, E., and D. Ames. "Changing Places: American Urban Policy for the 1990's." *Journal of Urban Affairs* 14, No. 3 (1992): 399–422.

Bronfenbrenner, Uri. "Ecology of the Family as Context for Human Development: Research Perspectives." *Developmental Psychology* 22 (1986): 723–742.

Bullard, Robert D., and Joe R. Feagin. "Racism and the City." In *Urban Life in Transition, Urban Affairs Annual Reviews* 39, eds. M. Gottdiener and Chris Pickvance. Newbury Park, Calif.: Sage Publications, 1991.

Chant, Sylvia. "Single-Parent Families: Choice or Constraint: The Formation of Female-headed Households in Mexican Shanty Towns." *Development and Change* 16 (1985): 649.

Comer, James, and H. Hill. "Social Policy and the Mental Health of Black Children." *Journal of the American Academy of Child Psychiatry* 24 (1985): 175–181.

Crow, Gary. *The Nurturing Family*. Milbrae, Calif.: Celestial Arts, 1980.

Danzinger, Sheldon H., and Daniel H. Weinburg, eds. *Fighting Poverty*. Cambridge, Mass.: Harvard University Press, 1986.

Dobash, R. Emerson, and Russell Dobash. *Violence Against Wives: A Case Against the Patriarchy*. London: Open Books, 1980.

Dolbeare, Cushing N. *Out of Reach, Why Everyday People Can't Find Affordable Housing*. Washington, D.C.: Low Income Housing Information Service, 1991.

Downs, A. *Opening Up the Suburbs*. New Haven, Conn.: Yale University Press, 1973.

Dreier, Peter. "Bush to Cities: Drop Dead," *The Progressive* 56, No. 7 (July 1992): 20–23.

Dreier, Peter, and Richard Applebaum. "The Housing Crisis Enters the 1990's." *New England Journal of Public Policy* 8, No. 1 (Spring/Summer 1992): 155–167. Special Issue on Homelessness: New England and Beyond, ed. Padraig O'Malley.

Duncan, G., and W. Rodgers. "Single-Parent Families: Are Their Economic Problems Transitory or Persistent?" *Family Planning Perspectives* 19, No. 4 (1987): 171–178.

Ellwood, David. "The Changing Structure of American Families." *Journal of the American Planning Association* 59, No. 1 (Winter 1993): 3–8.

Ellwood, David. *Poor Support: Poverty in the American Family.* New York: Basic Books, 1988.

Faludi, Susan. *Backlash: The Undeclared War Against American Women.* New York: Crown Publishing, 1991.

Fischetti, Mark. "Future Shock Meets the Photonics Workplace." *Photonics* (August 1993): 66–74.

Freeman, H. "Psychiatric Aspects of Environmental Stress." *International Journal of Mental Health* 17 (1988): 13–23.

Garfinkel, Irwin, and Sara McLanahan. *Single Mothers and Their Children.* Washington, D.C.: Urban Institute Press, 1986.

Gelles, Richard J. *The Violent Home.* Beverly Hills, Calif.: Sage Publications, 1972.

Giddens, Anthony. *The Constitution of Society: Outline of a Theory of Structuration.* Oxford: Polity Press, 1984.

Gilderbloom, John I., and Richard P. Applebaum. *Rethinking Rental Housing.* Philadelphia: Temple University Press, 1988.

Goldsmith, William W., and Edward Blakely. *Separate Societies: Poverty and Inequality in U.S. Cities.* Philadelphia: Temple University Press, 1992.

Gondolf, Edward W. *Battered Women As Survivors: An Alternative to Treating Learned Helplessness.* Lexington, Mass.: Lexington Books, 1988.

Googins, Bradley. *Work/Family Conflicts: Private Lives—Public Responses.* New York: Auburn House Publishing Co., 1991.

Gorov, Linda. "A Family Picture Framed by Violence." *The Boston Globe,* June 24, 1993, pp. 25 and 31.

Gottdiener, M., and Chris G. Pickvance, eds. *Urban Life in Transition, Urban Affairs Annual Reviews* 39. Newbury Park, Calif.: Sage Publications, 1991.

Gruen, Nina, and Claude Gruen. *Low and Moderate Income Housing in the Suburbs.* New York: Praeger, 1972.

Hanlon, Sydney. "Saving Battered Women." *The Boston Globe,* December 30, 1992.

Harvard Business Review 71, No. 5, September/October 1993, pp. 10–11.

Harvard University School of Public Health. "Report on Domestic Violence: A Commitment to Action," Boston: Harvard University Press, June 1993.

Hassett, J., and K. White. *Psychology in Perspective.* 2nd ed. New York: Harper and Row, 1989.

Hayden, Dolores. *Redesigning the American Dream: The Future of Housing, Work and Family Life.* New York: W. W. Norton, 1984.

Hewlett, Sylvia Ann. *When the Bough Breaks: The Cost of Neglecting Our Children.* New York: Basic Books, 1991.

Hohler, Bob. "Family Violence Report Urges Reforms." *The Boston Globe,* June 1, 1993, pp. 13 and 18.

Hohler, Bob. "State Domestic Violence Programs Need Overhaul, Harshberger Says." *The Boston Globe*, June 2, 1993, p. 21.

Hughes, Mark Alan. "Concentrated Deviance and the 'Underclass' Hypothesis." *Journal of Policy Analysis and Management* 8 (1989): 274–281.

Hughes, Mark Alan. "Misspeaking Truth to Power: A Geographical Perspective on the 'Underclass' Fallacy." *Economic Geography* 65, No. 3 (July 1989): 187–207.

Hughes, Mark Alan. "Employment Decentralization and Accessibility: A Strategy for Stimulating Regional Mobility." *Journal of the American Planning Association* 57, No. 3 (Summer 1991): 288–298.

Janssen, Bruce. *The Reluctant Welfare State.* 2nd ed. Pacific Grove, Calif.: Brooks/Cole Publishing Co., 1993.

Jargowsky, Paul A., and Mary Jo Bane. "Neighborhood Poverty: Basic Questions." Working paper series, Malcolm Wiener Center for Social Policy, John F. Kennedy School of Government, Harvard University, March 2, 1990.

Jencks, Christopher. "Is the American Underclass Growing?" In *The Urban Underclass*, eds. C. Jencks and P. Peterson. Washington, D.C.: Brookings Institution, 1991.

Jencks, Christopher. *Rethinking Social Policy: Race, Poverty and the Underclass.* Cambridge, Mass.: Harvard University Press, 1992.

Kamerman, Sheila B., and Alfred J. Kahn. *The Responsive Workplace: Employers and a Changing Labor Force.* New York: Columbia University Press, 1987.

Kamerman, Sheila B., and Alfred J. Kahn. *Mothers Alone: Strategies for a Time of Change.* Dover, Mass.: Auburn House Publishing Co., 1988.

Kamerman, Sheila B., and Alfred J. Kahn. "What Europe Does for Single-Parent Families." *The Public Interest*, 1989, pp. 70–86.

Kaplan, Sally, J. "Consequences of Sexual Harassment in the Workplace." *Affilia* 6, No. 3 (Fall 1991): 51–52.

Kornbluh, Felicia. "Women, Work, and Welfare in the '90s." *Social Policy* 21, No. 4 (Spring 1991): 23–39.

Kotlowitz, Alex. *There Are No Children Here: A Story of Two Boys Growing Up in the Other America.* New York: Doubleday Publishing Co., 1991.

Lake, Robert W. "Rethinking NIMBY." *American Planning Association Journal* 59, No. 1 (Winter 1993): 87–93.

Land, Hilary. "Time to Care." In *Women's Issues in Social Policy*, eds. Mavis MacLean and Duicie Groves. London: Routledge, 1991.

Lane, Terry, and Elizabeth Mulroy. "Analysis of the REACH Program, 1988–1992: A Study of an Emergency Housing Program for Homeless Pregnant Women." Prepared for Crittenton Hastings House, Boston, 1993.

Langen, Patrick A., and Christopher A. Innes. "Preventing Domestic Violence Against Women." U.S. Department of Justice, Bureau of Justice Statistics, NCJ-102037. Washington, D.C.: U.S. Government Printing Office, August 1986.

Leavitt, Jacqueline. "The Shelter-Service Crisis and Single Parents." In *The Unsheltered Woman: Women and Housing in the 1980's*, ed. Eugenie Birch. New Brunswick, N.J.: Center for Urban Policy Research, 1985.

Leinberger, Christopher. "Business Flees to the Urban Fringe." *The Nation* 255, No. 1 (1992): 10–14.

Linsky, Arnold, and Murray Straus. *Social Stress in the United States: Links to Regional Patterns in Crime and Illness*. Dover, Mass.: Auburn House Publishing Co., 1986.

Longres, John. *Human Behavior in the Social Environment*. Itasca, Ill.: Peacock Publishers, 1990.

Loprest, P. "Gender Differences in Wage Growth and Job Mobility." *The American Economic Review* 87 (1992): 526–532.

Maclean, Mavis, and Lenore Weitzman, eds. *Economic Consequences of Divorce: The International Perspective*. Oxford, England: Clarendon Press, 1992.

Massachusetts Coalition for the Homeless vs. Dukakis. Affidavit of Matthew P. Dumont, M.D., Suffolk Superior Court, Civil No. 80109, May 5, 1986, pp. 4–6.

McDowell, Linda. "Restructuring Production and Reproduction: Some Theoretical and Empirical Issues Relating to Gender, of Women in Britain." In *Urban Life in Transition, Urban Affairs Annual Reviews* 39, eds. M. Gottdiener and C. Pickvance. Newbury Park, Calif.: Sage Publications, 1991.

McGoldrick, Monica, and Betty Carter, eds. *The Changing Family Life Cycle*. Boston: Allyn and Bacon, 1989.

Meehan, Edward J. *The Quality of Federal Policy Making: Programmed Failure in Public Housing*. Columbia: University of Missouri Press, 1979.

Mendez, Helen A. "Single-Parent Families: A Topology of Life Styles." *Social Work* 24 (May 1979): 193–200.

Minuchin, Salvador. *Families and Family Therapy*. Cambridge, Mass.: Harvard University Press, 1974.

Moos, R., and B. Moos. *Life Stressors and Social Resources Inventory Preliminary Manual*. Palo Alto, Calif.: Social Ecology Laboratory, Stanford University and Veterans' Administrative Medical Center, 1990.

Morrill, M. A. "A Boston Townhouse." *Victorian Homes* (Winter 1993): 35–40.

Mulroy, Elizabeth A. "The Search for Affordable Housing." In *Women As Single Parents: Confronting Institutional Barriers in the Courts, the Workplace, and the Housing Market*, ed. Elizabeth A. Mulroy. Dover, Mass.: Auburn House Publishing Co., 1988.

Mulroy, Elizabeth A. "Mixed-Income Housing in Action." *Urban Land* 50, No. 5 (May 1991): 2–7.

Mulroy, Elizabeth A. "The Housing Affordability Slide in Action: How Single Mothers Slip into Homelessness." *New England Journal of Public Policy* 8, No. 1 (Spring/Summer 1992): 203–214. Special Issue on Homelessness: New England and Beyond.

Mulroy, Elizabeth A., and Terry S. Lane. "Housing Affordability, Stress and Single Mothers: Pathway to Homelessness." *Journal of Sociology and Social Welfare* 19, No. 3 (September 1992): 51–64.

Murray, Charles. *Losing Ground.* New York: Basic Books, 1984.

Myerson, Martha, and Edward C. Banfield. *Politics, Planning and the Public Interest: The Case of Public Housing in Chicago.* Glencoe, Ill.: Free Press, 1955.

National Victim Center. "Domestic Violence." INFOLINK, Vol. 1, No. 14, 1992.

Newman, O. *Community of Interest.* Garden City, N.Y.: Anchor Press/Doubleday, 1980.

Newsweek, October 11, 1993, p. 34.

O'Hare, William P. "America's Minorities—The Demographics of Diversity." *Population Bulletin* 47, No. 4, Population Reference Bureau (December 1992): 25.

O'Regan, Katherine and John Quigley. "Labor Market Access and Labor Market Outcomes for Urban Youth." *Regional Science and Urban Economics* 21 (1991): 277–292.

Perin, Constance. *Everything in Its Place: Social Order and Land Use in America.* Princeton, N.J.: Princeton University Press, 1977.

Polikoff, Alexander. *Housing the Poor: The Case for Heroism.* Cambridge, Mass.: Ballinger Press, 1978.

Prowthrow-Stith, Deborah. *Deadly Consequences.* New York: Harper Collins, 1991.

Pynoos, Jon, Robert Schafer, and Chester Hartman, eds. *Housing Urban America.* 2nd ed. New York: Aldine Publishing, 1980.

Radigan, Anne L. "Federal Policy-making and Family Issues." In *Women As Single Parents: Confronting Institutional Barriers in the Courts, the Workplace, and the Housing Market,* ed. Elizabeth A. Mulroy. Dover, Mass.: Auburn House Publishing Co., 1988.

Rawlings, Steve. "Single Parents and Their Children." U.S. Bureau of the Census. "Studies in Marriage and the Family." *Current Population Reports,* Series P-23, No. 162. Washington, D.C.: U.S. Government Printing Office, 1989.

Rein, Martin, et al. "The Impact of Family Change on Housing Careers." Unpublished report prepared for the Department of Housing and Urban Development by the Joint Center for Urban Studies, Cambridge, Mass., 1980.

Richards, L. "The Precarious Survival and Hard-Won Satisfactions of White Single Parent Families." *Family Relations* 38 (1989): 396–403.

Ricketts, E. R., and I. Sawhill. "Defining and Measuring the Underclass." *Journal of Policy Analysis and Management* 7 (1988): 316–325.

Roberts, Bryan R. "Household Coping Strategies and Urban Poverty in a Comparative Perspective." In *Urban Life in Transition, Urban Affairs Annual Reviews* 39, eds. M. Gottdiener and Chris G. Pickvance. Newbury Park, Calif.: Sage Publications, 1991.

Rohe, W. "Urban Planning and Mental Health." *Prevention in Human Services* 4 (1985): 79–110.

Rosenbaum, James, and Susan Popkin. "The Gautreaux Program: An Experiment in Racial and Economic Integration." *The Center Report: Current Policy Issues 2*, No. 1 (Spring 1990): 4. Evanston, Ill.: Northwestern University.

Rosenbaum, James, and Susan Popkin. "Economic and Social Impacts of Housing Integration." *Research and Policy Reports*, Center for Urban Affairs and Policy Research. Evanston, Ill.: Northwestern University, March 1990.

Ross, Heather, and Isabel Sawhill. *Time of Transition: The Growth of Families Headed by Women.* Washington, D.C.: Urban Institute, 1975.

Rutter, M. "Psychosocial Resilience and Protective Mechanisms." *American Journal of Orthopsychiatry* 57 (1987): 316–331.

Saluter, Arlene. "Singleness in America." U.S. Bureau of the Census, "Studies in Marriage and the Family." *Current Population Reports*, Series P-23, No. 162. Washington, D.C.: U.S. Government Printing Office, 1989.

Sard, Barbara. "Housing the Homeless Through Expanding Access to Existing Housing Subsidies." *New England Journal of Public Policy* (Spring/Summer 1992): 187–201. Special Issue on Homelessness, New England and Beyond.

Schafran, Lynn Hecht. "Gender Bias in the Courts." In *Women As Single Parents: Confronting Institutional Barriers in the Courts, the Workplace, and the Housing Market*, ed. Elizabeth A. Mulroy. Dover, Mass.: Auburn Housing Publishing Co., 1988.

Schechter, Susan, and Lisa Gary. "Understanding and Empowering Battered Women." In *Abuse and Victimization Across the Life Span*, ed. M. B. Straus. Baltimore, Md.: Johns Hopkins University Press, 1988.

Short, John R. *The Humane City.* Oxford, England: Basil Blackwell Ltd., 1989.

Sidel, Ruth. *Women and Children Last: The Plight of Poor Women in Affluent America.* New York: Viking Penguin, 1987.

Smizik, Frank I., and Michael E. Stone. "Single-Parent Families and a Right to Housing." *Women as Single Parents: Confronting Institutional Barriers in the Courts, the Workplace, and the Housing Market*, ed. Elizabeth A. Mulroy. Dover, Mass.: Auburn House Publishing Co., 1988.

Sommers, Albert T. "The U.S. Economy: A New American 'Normal'." *Across the Board.* The Conference Board, December 1992, pp. 26–32.

Sorrentino, Constance. "The Changing Family in International Perspective." *Monthly Labor Review* 113, No. 3 (March 1990): 41–58.

Steinmetz, S. *The Cycle of Violence: Assertive, Aggressive, and Abusive Family Interaction*. New York: Praeger, 1977.

Stoesz, David. "The Fall of the Industrial City: The Reagan Legacy for Urban Policy." *Journal of Sociology and Social Welfare* 19, No. 1 (1992): 149–167. Special Issue on the Reagan Legacy and the American Welfare State.

Stone, Michael. *Shelter Poverty: New Ideas on Affordable Housing*. Philadelphia: Temple University Press, 1993.

Straus, Murray. "Wife Beating: How Common and Why?" *Victimology* 2 (1978).

Straus, Murray A., ed. *Abuse and Victimization Across the Life Span*. Baltimore, Md.: Johns Hopkins University Press, 1988.

Straus, Murray, and Richard Gelles. "Societal Changes in Family Violence from 1975 to 1985." *Journal of Marriage and the Family* 48 (1986).

The United Nations. *Women: Challenges in the Year 2000*. New York: United Nations Department of Public Information, 1991.

U.S. Bureau of the Census. "The Black Population in the United States: March 1990 and 1989." *Current Population Reports*, Series P-20, No. 448. Washington, D.C.: U.S. Government Printing Office, 1990.

U.S. Bureau of the Census. "Household and Family Characteristics: March 1990 and 1989." *Current Population Reports*, Series P-20, No. 447. Washington, D.C.: U.S. Government Printing Office, 1990.

U.S. Bureau of the Census. "Housing Characteristics of Selected Races and Hispanic-Origin Households in the United States: 1987." Series H121-87-1. Washington, D.C.: U.S. Government Printing Office, 1990.

U.S. Bureau of the Census. "Marital Status and Living Arrangements: March 1990." *Current Population Reports*, Series P-20, No. 450. Washington, D.C.: U.S. Government Printing Office, 1991.

U.S. Bureau of the Census. "Household and Family Characteristics: 1991." *Current Population Reports*, Series P-20, No. 458. Washington, D.C.: U.S. Government Printing Office, 1992.

U.S. Bureau of the Census. "Money Income of Households, Families, and Persons in the United States: 1990." *Current Population Reports*, Series P-60, No. 174. Washington, D.C.: U.S. Government Printing Office, 1991.

U.S. Department of Health and Human Services. "Family Violence: An Overview." Office of Human Development Services, Office of Policy, Planning and Legislation. Washington, D.C.: U.S. Government Printing Office, 1991.

U.S. Department of Labor, Bureau of Labor Statistics. "Employment in Perspective: Women in the Labor Force." Report 822, Fourth Quarter. Washington, D.C.: U.S. Government Printing Office, 1991.

Veum, J., and P. Gleason. "Child Care: Arrangements and Costs." *Monthly Labor Review* 114, No. 10 (1991): 10–17.

Waring, Nancy. "Who's Delinquent?" *The Boston Globe Magazine*, October 17, 1993, p. 16.

Wasoff, Frances, and Rebecca Dobash. "Moving the Family: Changing Housing Circumstances After Divorce." In *Housing and Divorce*, Studies in Housing No. 4, ed. Peter Symon. Center for Housing Research, University of Glasgow, Scotland, 1990, pp. 139–166.

Weitzman, Lenore J. *The Divorce Revolution: The Unexpected Social and Economic Consequences for Women and Children in America*. New York: Free Press, 1985.

Wilkie, Jane Riblett. "The Decline in Men's Labor Force Participation and Income and the Changing Structure of Family Economic Support." *Journal of Marriage and the Family* 53, No. 1 (February 1991): 111–122.

Wilson, William Julius. *The Truly Disadvantaged: The Inner City, the Underclass, and Public Policy*. Chicago: University of Chicago Press, 1987.

Wilson, William Julius. "Academic Controversy and Intellectual Growth." In *Social Lives*, ed. Matilda White Riley. Newbury Park, Calif.: Sage Publications, 1988.

Wolch, Jennifer, and Michael Dear. *Malign Neglect: Homelessness in an American City*. San Francisco: Jossey-Bass Inc., Publishers, 1993.

Wolch, Jennifer R., Michael Dear, and Andrea Akita. "Explaining Homelessness." *Journal of the American Planning Association* 54, No. 4 (Autumn 1988): 443–453.

Index

About the Author

ELIZABETH A. MULROY is Associate Professor at the School of Social Work, University of Hawaii at Manoa. She is one of the nation's leading experts on housing and poverty policy. Among her earlier publications is *Women As Single Parents* (Auburn House, 1988).

ISBN 0-86569-038-3

EAN

9 780865 690387

HARDCOVER BAR CODE

90000>